FROM THE MARGINS

LEE KRASNER | NORMAN LEWIS

1945–1952

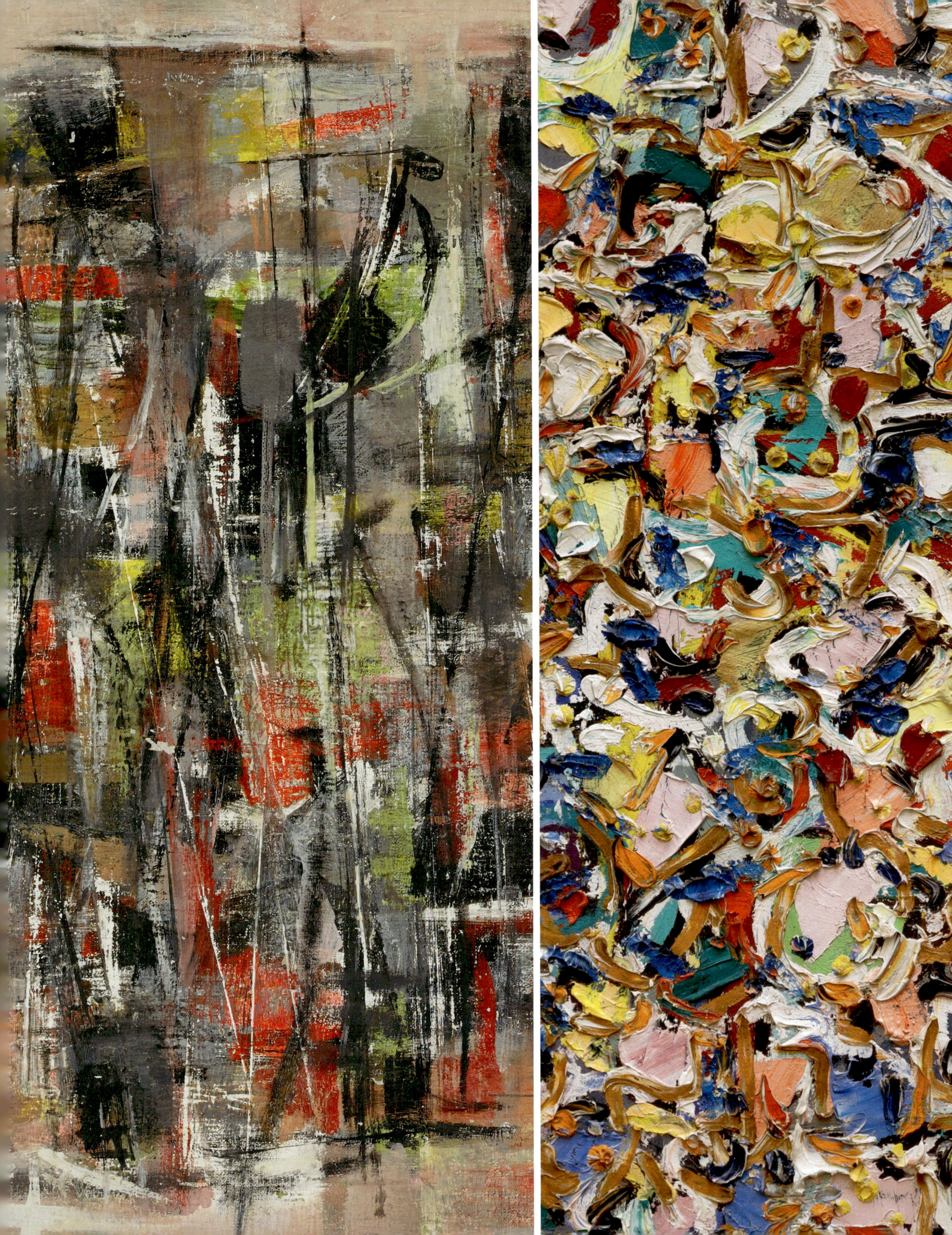

FROM THE MARGINS

LEE KRASNER | NORMAN LEWIS
1945–1952

norman l. kleeblatt and **stephen brown**

with essays by lisa saltzman and mia l. bagneris

THE JEWISH MUSEUM, NEW YORK

UNDER THE AUSPICES OF THE
JEWISH THEOLOGICAL SEMINARY

DISTRIBUTED BY
YALE UNIVERSITY PRESS
NEW HAVEN AND LONDON

This book has been published in conjunction with the exhibition *From the Margins: Lee Krasner | Norman Lewis, 1945–1952*, organized by The Jewish Museum, New York, September 12, 2014–February 1, 2015.

Artwork copyright notices and photograph credits appear on page 96.

Director of Publications: Eve Sinaiko
Edited by Harriet Whelchel
Designed by Steven Schoenfelder
Typeset in Univers and Futura by
Jennifer Sugden
Proofread by Carrie Wicks and Sylvia Karchmar

Produced by Marquand Books, Inc., Seattle
marquand.com

The Jewish Museum
1109 Fifth Avenue
New York, NY 10128
thejewishmuseum.org

Distributed by
Yale University Press
302 Temple Street
P.O. Box 209040
New Haven, CT 06520-9040
yalebooks.com/art

Library of Congress Control Number:
2014930324

ISBN 978-0-300-20649-4

The paper for this book meets the guidelines for permanence and durability of the Committee on Production Guidelines for Book Longevity of the Council on Library Resources.

10 9 8 7 6 5 4 3 2 1

Color management by iocolor, Seattle
Printed and bound in China by
Artron Color Printing, Ltd.

On the cover: decorative motifs based on details from Lee Krasner, *Untitled*, 1948 (see page 32), and Norman Lewis, *Jazz Band*, 1948 (see page 83).

Frontispiece: detail of Norman Lewis, *Untitled*, 1949 (left), see page 51; Lee Krasner, *Noon*, 1947 (right), see page 50.

Page 8: detail of Lee Krasner, *Untitled*, 1949 (left), see page 69; Norman Lewis, *Just Firmament*, 1951 (right), see page 22.

Page 10: detail of Norman Lewis, *Every Atom Glows: Electrons in Luminous Vibration*, 1951 (left), see page 61; Lee Krasner, *Lava*, 1950 (right), see page 60.

CONTENTS

THE JEWISH MUSEUM BOARD OF TRUSTEES

DONORS AND LENDERS TO THE EXHIBITION

DONORS

The exhibition is made possible in part by The Peter Jay Sharp Exhibition Fund and The Pollock-Krasner Foundation. Endowment support is provided by The Skirball Fund for American Jewish Life Exhibitions.

LENDERS

Birmingham Museum of Art

Betty A. Davis, New York

Delaware Art Museum, Wilmington

Caryn and Craig Effron

Elisha Hawkins Collection of African American and African Art

Tarin M. Fuller, Newark

halley k harrisburg and Michael Rosenfeld, New York

The Jewish Museum, New York

Nancy Margolis King

Pamela J. Joyner/Alfred J. Giuffrida

The Estate of Norman W. Lewis

Raymond J. McGuire

The Metropolitan Museum of Art, New York

Robert Miller Gallery

Rodney M. Miller

Museum of Fine Arts, Boston

The Museum of Modern Art, New York

Philadelphia Museum of Art

The Pollock-Krasner Foundation, New York

Private collections

Michael Rosenfeld Gallery, New York

Saint Louis Art Museum

Studio Museum in Harlem

Virginia Museum of Fine Arts

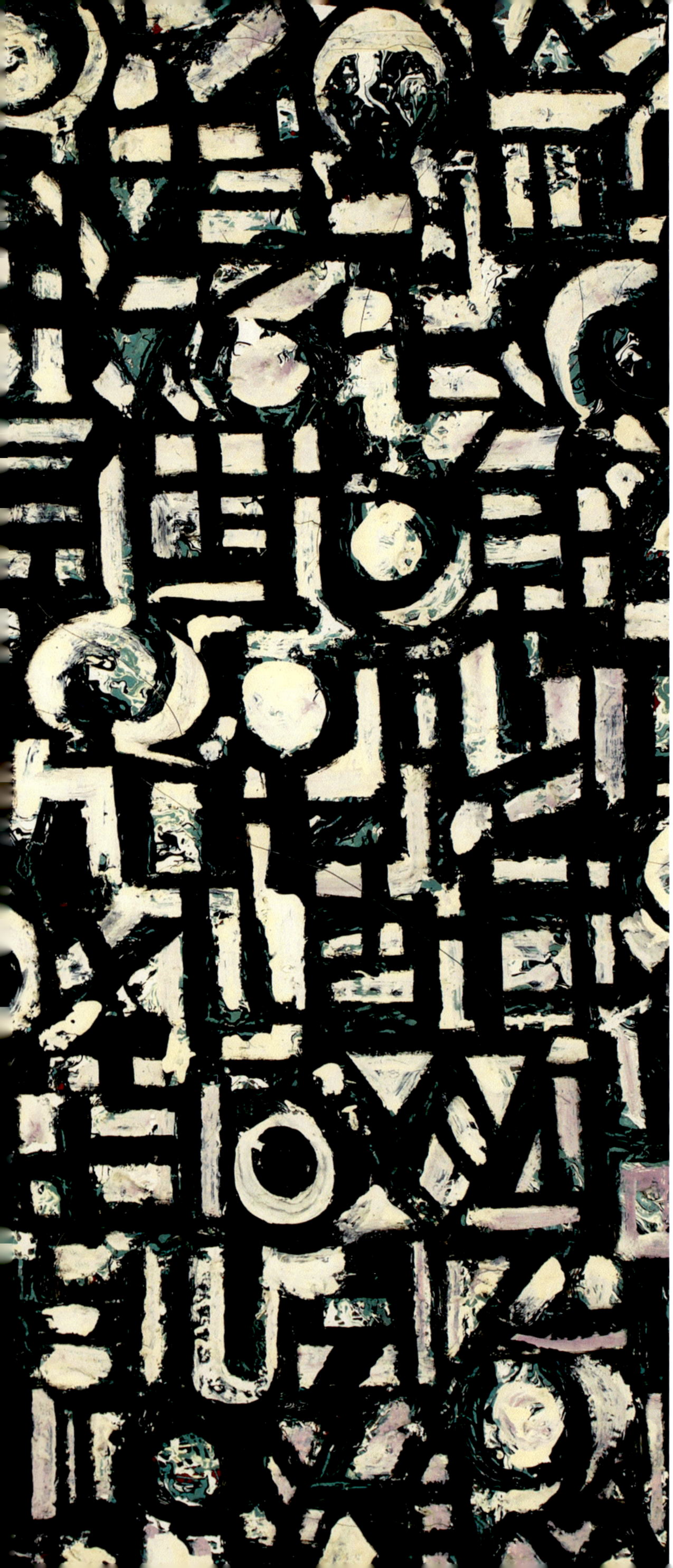

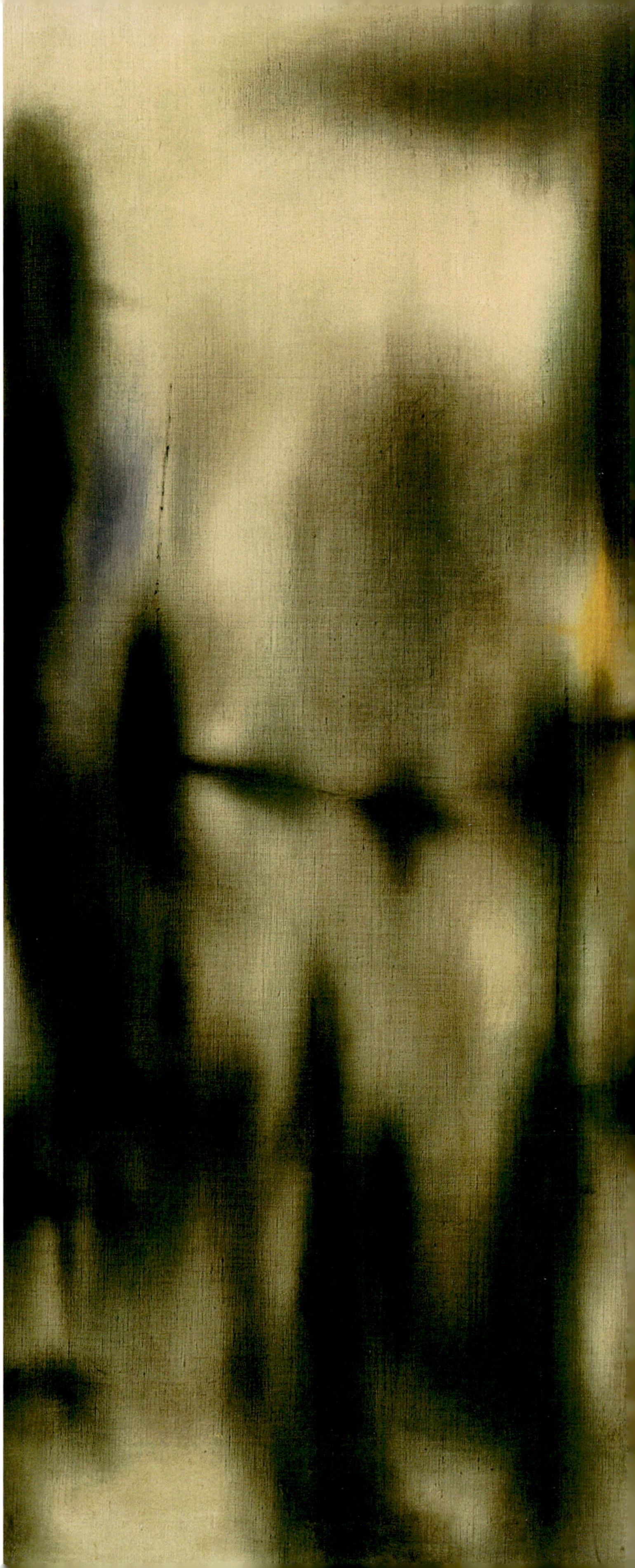

FOREWORD

Mounting an exhibition is a long, complex curatorial process. The position of each work of art is carefully considered and its relationship to other works within a gallery discussed at length. Even so, serendipity plays a role: unplanned, interesting juxtapositions can occur—and every good curator hopes that they will.

When The Jewish Museum presented *Action/Abstraction: Pollock, De Kooning, and American Art, 1940–1976* in 2008, the art of Lee Krasner and Norman Lewis was shown in the context of their more famous colleagues. The subtle pleasures of their work shone through—as did an unexpected sense that the paintings of these two had a great deal to say to one another. This was the genesis of the present exhibition.

It is always a particular pleasure to show work that has not been widely seen before. Many of the works in *From the Margins* come from private collections; others are from large institutions but are often not on display. Here, then, is a chance for visitors to see abstract expressionist paintings that are intimate and personal, presented in our elegant second-floor galleries, which still retain the proportions and decorative details of a private home. In such a setting, Krasner and Lewis's abstractions reveal intriguing complexities of style, iconography, and rhythm, relationships to jazz, to calligraphy, and to politics that are deeply satisfying. The "conversation" between them that began six years ago is now expanded.

We are deeply grateful to our lenders—the more so as they are sharing with us many works not readily available to the public. We thank our donors and funders, whose stalwart generosity is a mainstay of the museum's exhibition program. As ever, our Board of Trustees has demonstrated its dedication to the exploration of modern art, from the splendid and spectacular to its quieter corners.

My thanks to Norman L. Kleeblatt and Stephen Brown, whose insightful curatorial work has led to an exhibition of great elegance and beauty. We were fortunate to have exceptional assistants on this project: Grace Astrove, Chana Boruchov, Talya Feldman, Tori Meyer, and Soomin Shon, curatorial interns; and Daniel Roza, Blanksteen Curatorial Fellow. To all of them I extend my gratitude.

claudia gould
HELEN GOLDSMITH MENSCHEL DIRECTOR
THE JEWISH MUSEUM

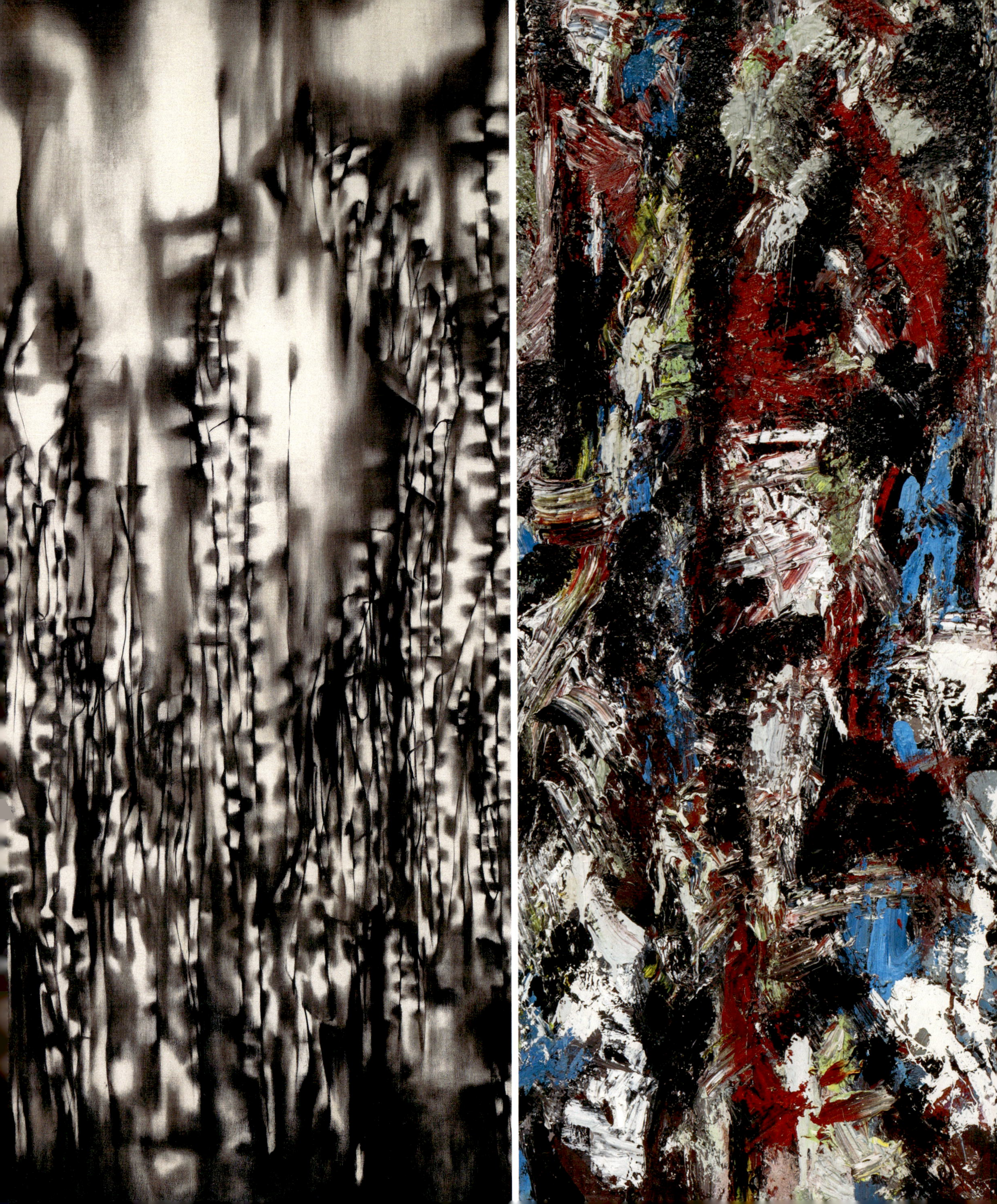

PREFACE AND ACKNOWLEDGMENTS

Norman Lewis's *Twilight Sounds* (1947) and Lee Krasner's *Untitled* (1948) were two of the more modestly scaled paintings included in *Action/Abstraction: Pollock, De Kooning, and American Art, 1940–1976*, an exhibition presented at this museum several years ago. Without seeming to struggle for visibility against the range of large-scale masterworks of the period that surrounded them, the paired paintings (pages 32, 33) captured the attention of numerous viewers. Long after the show's close, curators, collectors, and critics remarked on their unanticipated synergy. It seemed as if some compelling relation existed between these lesser-known lights of abstract expressionism. Discussion with colleagues at the museum and beyond suggested that it might be of interest to widen the focus on these two artists, particularly during the first flowering of their abstract styles in the 1940s and early 1950s. Whereas the earlier exhibition may have appeared symphonic—set within the context of the critical rivalry between Clement Greenberg and Harold Rosenberg and manifest in a wide variety of paintings, sculpture, and mass media created by more than thirty artists over a thirty-five year period—the current juxtaposition of works by these two artists seems more akin to chamber music.

From the Margins: Lee Krasner | Norman Lewis, 1945–1952 brings together the paintings of these two representatives of the New York School, who made significant contributions through their unique and compelling approaches to abstract art. Virtually excluded from the critical discourse of their times, they represent an intriguing rapport—in terms of form and what might be called personal iconographies. The comparison of works by Krasner, a Jewish American woman, and by Lewis, an African American man—provides for a fascinating dynamic. The various consonances with regard to image and text within Krasner's approach to abstraction are brought together in this volume by Lisa Saltzman, who pieces together the elements of the painter's visual code, which in effect represents Krasner's search for an artistic style. As Mia Bagneris demonstrates in her contribution to this book, the work of Lewis—in the richness of its formal concerns, its nocturnal references, and its evocation of locale—is enhanced by an understanding of the painter's sense of his own artistic persona.

At its heart, the exhibition juxtaposes Krasner's so-called Little Image paintings with the Little Figure paintings of Lewis. The former, suggestive of glyphs or calligraphy, have been considered in connection with Krasner's background, her study of Hebrew, and her interest in other types of script. In his Little Figure paintings, Lewis riffs on aspects of his particular cultural heritage, including, among other themes, Harlem street life, patterns in African textiles, jazz, and jazz musicians. In these works the artists were transforming their respective practices, creating paintings intense with gesture, incident, and associations—laying the groundwork for their later achievements. The art of Lee Krasner and Norman Lewis during the 1940s and early 1950s offers a fascinating counterpoint—a play of themes and variations leading to the creation of impressive works, which in turn offer intriguing points of departure for the exploration of modern painterly abstraction.

This publication and the exhibition that it accompanies have depended on the assistance and cooperation of many institutions and private individuals. We are very grateful for the support of colleagues at The Jewish Museum, in particular Jens Hoffmann, Deputy Director; Ruth Beesch, Deputy Director; Julie Maguire, Senior Registrar; and Jennifer Ayres, Exhibitions Coordinator. Important support for the project on a variety of administrative tasks and research initiatives has been provided by Karen Levitov, former Associate Curator; Marni Corbett in the Development department; Grace Astrove, Chana Boruchov, Talya Feldman, Tori Meyer, and Soomin Shon, curatorial interns; and Daniel Roza, Blanksteen Curatorial Fellow. We are also grateful for significant help from the museum's volunteers, in particular Sally Lindenbaum. Ella Levitt conducted valuable outside research on materials related to both artists. Deep thanks are owed to the chair of the Board, to the Trustees, and to Claudia Gould, Helen Goldsmith Menschel Director, for their interest in this presentation of two parallel and fascinating oeuvres.

We are most grateful to Lisa Saltzman and to Mia Bagneris for their thoughtful contributions to this volume, to Harriet Whelchel for her careful and perceptive editing of the texts, and to Eve Sinaiko, Director of Publications, for expertise she brought to this project.

An immense team of professionals is required to produce any exhibition, and we must thank in general terms all those who have contributed their skills and efforts. To the conservators who have ensured the integrity of the works; to the architect, Dan Kershaw, and his team; to Steven Schoenfelder, graphic designer; to the staff at Marquand Books; and to the museum's development, communications, technical, and operations staff, led by Al Lazarte, we offer our warm appreciation. The photographers Marc Bernier, Erik Gould, Ian Reeves, Brad Robotham, and above all David Heald provided superb work.

We have benefited in myriad ways from other friends and colleagues beyond the museum who must be mentioned for their suggestions, aid, and support: Catherine Craft, Lewis Kachur, and Noriko Matsumoto. We hope they will recognize how grateful we are for their role in this project.

It is impossible to adequately express appreciation to the lenders to this exhibition for their extraordinary generosity, but we offer hearty and enthusiastic thanks to all of them for their willing participation.

We are indebted to several libraries and archives for the use of their resources and for assistance, in particular the Columbia University Libraries and Avery Fine Arts and Architectural Library and the Schomburg Center for Research in Black Culture of the New York Public Library.

Finally, we express deep appreciation to the many individuals who have provided valuable assistance with loans and documentation: Matthew Affron, Philadelphia Museum of Art; Matthew Bailey, John and Susan Horseman Collection; Charles C. Bergman, The Pollock-Krasner Foundation; Graham C. Boettcher, Birmingham Museum of Art; Jonathan Boos; Mark Borghi; Kerrie Buitrago, The Pollock-Krasner Foundation; Cyanne T. Chutkow, Christie's; Harry Cooper, National Gallery of Art; Robert Cozzolino, Pennsylvania Academy of the Fine Arts; Heather Coyle, Delaware Art Museum; Marjorie Van Cura, Michael Rosenfeld Gallery; Gregg Deering, Atelier 4; Leslie Dressler, Museum of Fine Arts, Boston; Gwendolyn Dubois Shaw; Melvin Edwards; Ruth Fine; Nigel Freeman; Tarin M. Fuller; Elizabeth Goldberg, Sotheby's; Lily Goldberg, Museum of Modern Art; Jane Glaubinger; halley k harrisburg; Helen A. Harrison, Pollock-Krasner House; Barbara Haskell; Robert Hobbs; Billy E. and Navindren Hodges; John and Susan Horseman; Cynthia Iavarone, Metropolitan Museum of Art; Corrine Jennings; Ellen Landau; Tammi Lawson; Gail Levin; Ouida B. Lewis; Matthew Marks; Max Marshall; Crystal McCrary; Raymond J. McGuire; Jen Mergel, Museum of Fine Arts, Boston; Betsy Wittenborn Miller, Robert Miller Gallery; Lisbeth Murray; Harry Philbrick, Pennsylvania Academy of the Fine Arts; John Ravenal, Virginia Museum of Fine Arts; Rachel Rees, Christie's; Paul Richert-Garcia; Nina del Rio, Sotheby's; Kerry Rose, National Gallery of Art; Michael Rosenfeld; Samantha Shaffer, Christie's; Lowery Stokes Sims; Eugen Smetana; David Smith; Suzanne Stephens, Birmingham Museum of Art; Anne Temkin, Museum of Modern Art; Becca Tilghman, Metropolitan Museum of Art; Janeen Turk, Saint Louis Art Museum; Sheena Wagstaff, Metropolitan Museum of Art; Randy White, Robert Miller Gallery; Alison Whiting, Christie's; Shelley Wilson, Studio Museum in Harlem; Jason H. Wright; Roy Zuckerberg; Pamela Vander Zwan.

norman l. kleeblatt
SUSAN AND ELIHU ROSE CHIEF CURATOR

stephen brown
ASSISTANT CURATOR

INTRODUCTION: FROM THE MARGINS

Lee Krasner (1908–1984) and Norman Lewis (1909–1979) are increasingly recognized as important figures within abstract expressionism, and as the authors of major oeuvres, yet both are sparsely represented in the criticism of the period. In the exhibition titled *Action/Abstraction: Pollock, De Kooning, and American Art, 1940–1976*, organized by the Jewish Museum in 2008, the focus of the presentation concerned critical discourse during the period of abstract expressionism—in particular the defining views of Clement Greenberg and Harold Rosenberg. Although included in that exhibition, the works of Lee Krasner and Norman Lewis had to be grouped under a special rubric, indicative of a noticeable *lack* of critical reception: "Blind Spots."[1] Although it would be a failure to insist on a direct isometry, as contemporaries active within the same milieu, the artists' development during the 1940s and early 1950s suggests intriguing points of contact. In the formative years of the movement, both painters developed approaches that included many of the signature elements of the style—anti-representational concerns, a decentered, or allover approach to the picture plane, spontaneous or gestural brushwork, and a coloristic freedom from naturalistic effects. Their first engagements with abstraction were nevertheless accompanied by attention to extrapictorial references, along with a shared attachment to the use of line and a focus on works of modest scale. By contrast, the canvases that became iconic of the abstract movement in mid-twentieth-century America favored monumental, imposing statements to which universal signifi-

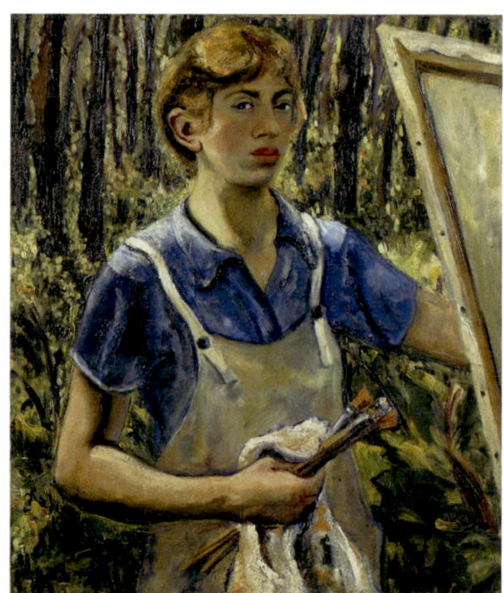

Lee Krasner, *Self-Portrait*, c. 1930.
Oil on linen, 30⅛ × 25⅛ in. (76.5 × 63.8 cm).
The Jewish Museum, New York. Purchase: Esther Leah Ritz Bequest; B. Gerald Cantor, Lady Kathleen Epstein, and Louis E. and Rosalyn M. Shecter Gifts, by exchange; Fine Arts Acquisitions Committee Fund; and Miriam Handler Fund.

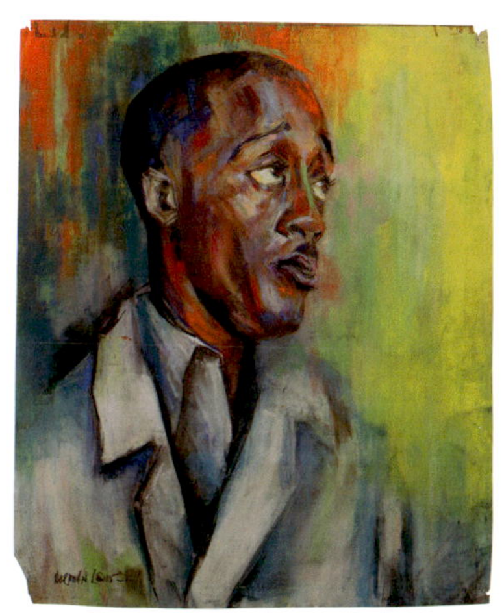

Norman Lewis, *Self-Portrait*, 1939.
Wax pastel and gouache on paper,
22¾ × 18½ in. (57.8 × 47 cm).
Collection of Tarin M. Fuller, Newark.

cance or transcendent meanings were often attached. The works of Willem de Kooning, Jackson Pollock, Clyfford Still, and others frequently overshadowed the creations of artists who would become recognized decades later by those more open to work by women and people of color.[2]

PORTRAITS OF THE ARTISTS Lee Krasner was born Lena Krassner to parents who had recently migrated from Russia to Brooklyn.[3] At the age of eighteen, she began studies at the Women's Art School of the Cooper Union. After spending the summer of 1928 at the Art Students League, she became a student at the National Academy of Design. Krasner continued to study art while supporting herself as an artist's model and waitress. In early 1934, she worked on the Public Works Art Project and in 1935 was attached as an artist to the Mural Division. Her participation lasted through the spring of 1943, when the Federal Art Project of the Works Progress Administration was subsumed by the government war effort.[4] Norman Lewis was the second of three sons of immigrant parents from Bermuda. His family lived on Lenox Avenue, near 132nd Street, in Harlem. Lewis studied drawing and commercial design in high school before joining the merchant marine and sailing through the Caribbean and off the coast of South America. Back in New York in the early 1930s, Lewis met Augusta Savage, the founder and director of an important art school, the Savage Studio of Arts and Crafts. From 1933 to 1935, he participated in Savage's studio and attended Columbia University. In 1936, Lewis also began work for the Federal Art Project.[5]

UNDER THE INFLUENCE During the 1930s, Krasner and Lewis worked in contemporary figurative styles influenced by social realism, cubism, and aspects of surrealism. The involvement of both artists in the federal arts programs provided training and allowed them access to cultural networks. Their work for the WPA, with its communal perspectives and collaborative projects, preceded their turns to the highly personal manners that would characterize their efforts during the 1940s. In 1937, Krasner began to study with Hans Hofmann, the German painter whose work and teachings, steeped in European modernism, had a significant influence on American art and aesthetics

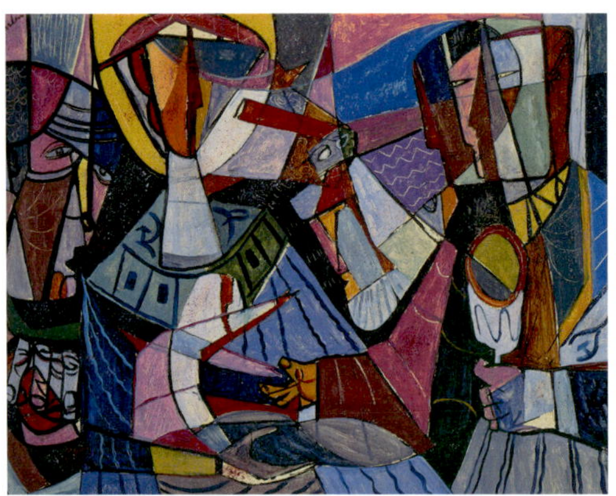

Romare Bearden, *Adoration of the Wise Men*, 1945. Oil on masonite, 22¼ × 28⅛ in. (56.5 × 71.4 cm). Newark Museum, Gift of Mr. and Mrs. Benjamin E. Tepper, 1946.

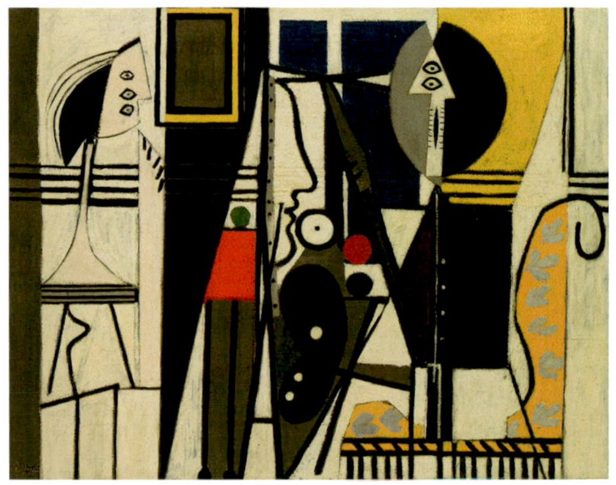

Pablo Picasso, *Painter and Model*, 1928. Oil on canvas, 51⅛ × 64¼ in. (129.8 × 163 cm). The Museum of Modern Art, New York, the Sidney and Harriet Janis Collection.

immediately before and after World War II. At the Hofmann School of Fine Arts, Krasner learned to experiment with abstract approaches to painting.

In addition to his work with the WPA, Lewis taught classes at the Harlem Community Arts Center, which he helped found in 1937, and at the George Washington Carver School. Lewis was a member of the artists' group 306, which met in the studios of Charles Alston, Henry Bannarn, and Ad Bates at 306 West 141st Street. The group formed a nucleus for creative life in Harlem and included Romare Bearden, Jacob Lawrence, Augusta Savage, and Richard Wright. The relationship between the artist and society was a frequent theme of discussion: yet from a style grounded in social realism, Lewis moved, during the early 1940s, toward abstraction—exploring the dissolution of the image while maintaining a tension between painting and reference. In his application for a Guggenheim Fellowship in 1949, Lewis wrote that art depended on ideas, "but this must be an aesthetic idea; the elements of painting constitute a language in themselves."[6]

The impact of cubism and the work of Pablo Picasso is apparent in the artistic development of both Krasner and Lewis, inflected by a use of color that joins the fragmentation implicit in cubist tectonics to the emotional trends associated with expressionism. The Museum of Modern Art in New York and its prominent exhibitions of the 1930s—in particular two shows mounted by Alfred H. Barr, *Cubism and Abstract Art* and *Fantastic Art, Dada, Surrealism* (both 1936)—affected both artists. For Lewis, the exhibition *African Negro Art*, organized by James Johnson Sweeney in the previous year, was a further inspiration. The painter Arshile Gorky, as well as Hofmann and the artist and writer John Graham, were influential in fostering Krasner's interest in Picasso.[7]

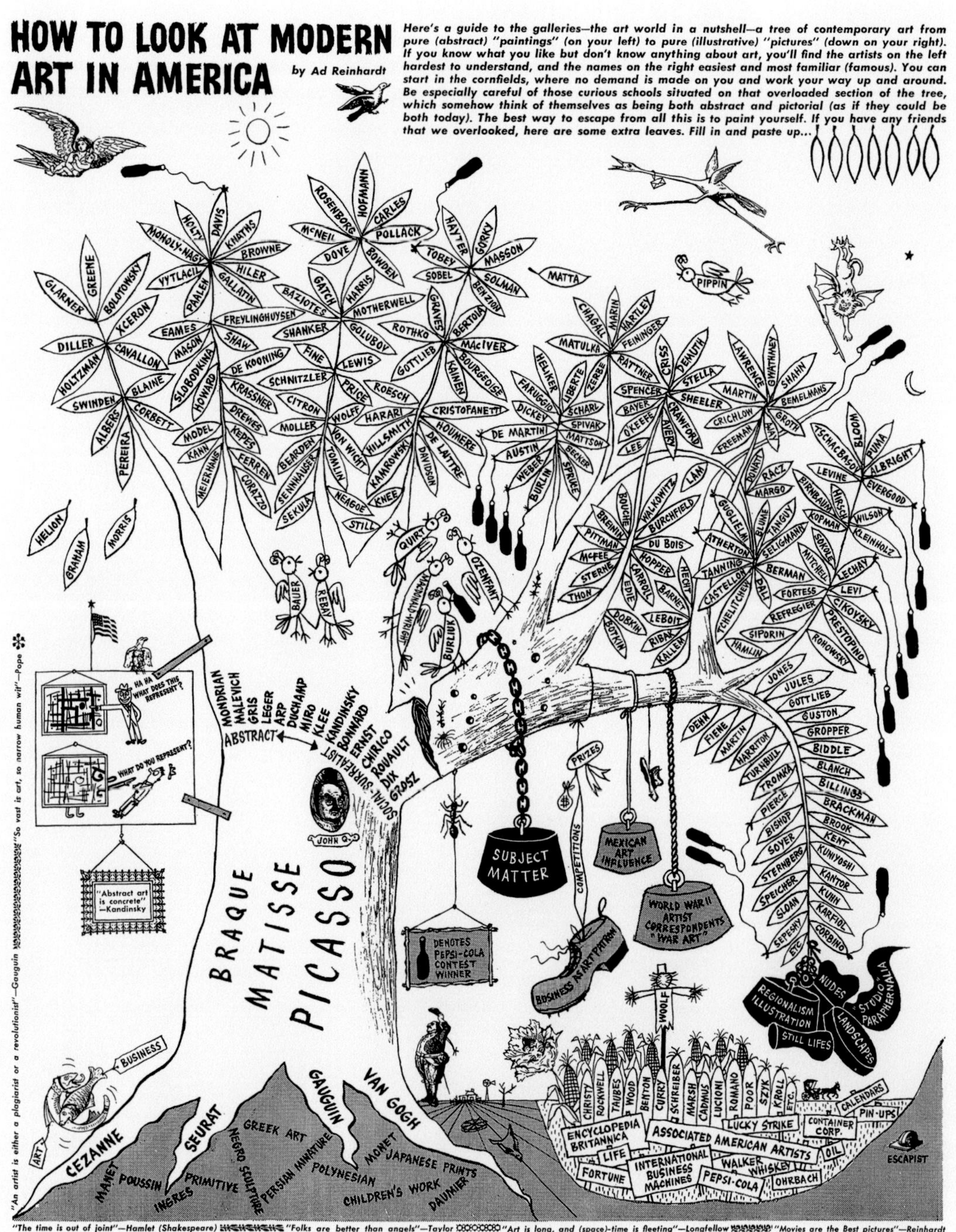

Ad Reinhardt, *How to Look at Modern Art in America*, published in *P.M.* magazine, June 2, 1946.

TOWARD ABSTRACTION An early influence, the painter Vaclav Vytlacil, brought Lewis into the orbit of the American Abstract Artists, a group that included Ad Reinhardt and Krasner.[8] The AAA held the formalist view that the elements of visual art (shape, composition, color) had expressive qualities per se. Reinhardt and Lewis, who had become friends, left their teaching positions, dependent on the Jefferson School of Social Science, due to their disaffection with social realism.[9] Reinhardt's take on where various artists stood in the effort toward abstraction is the subject of his satirical drawing *How to Look at Modern Art in America.* He imagines modern art as a tree whose trunk is emblazoned with the foundational names Georges Braque, Henri Matisse, and Picasso. Above them the tree has two branches, one sound and one that is cracking. At the base of the split is a row of other important artists' names, arranged in a range from "abstract" to "social-surrealist": Piet Mondrian, Marcel Duchamp, Joan Miró, Paul Klee, Wassily Kandinsky, and others. Above these, the breaking limb is weighed down by "subject matter," and sprouts leaves bearing names of more than one hundred artists, including Marc Chagall, Rockwell Kent, and Edward Hopper. A somewhat smaller group of leaves springs from the healthy branch; in the foliage are the names Krassner and Lewis.[10]

A geometric approach in the work of both artists coincided with their interest in constructive form, reminiscent of paintings such as Mondrian's *Broadway Boogie-Woogie*, 1942–43. In fact, Krasner knew Mondrian during his period of exile in New York and is recorded as an occasional dancing partner of the Dutch artist, whose interest in American culture extended to jazz and the rhythms of

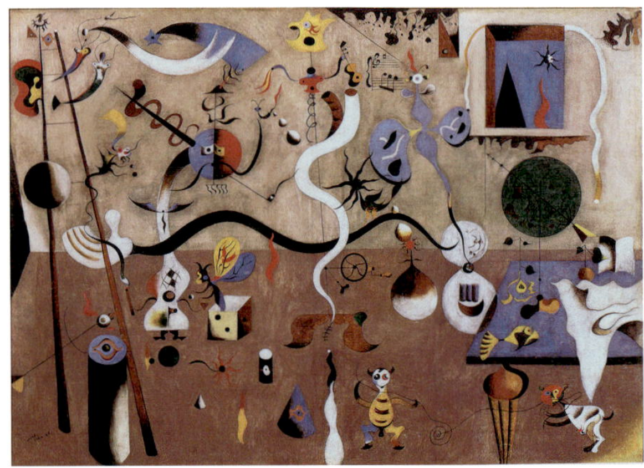

Joan Miró, *Carnival of Harlequin*, 1924–25. Oil on canvas, 26 × 35⅝ in. (66 × 90.5 cm). Albright-Knox Art Gallery, Buffalo, Room of Contemporary Art Fund, 1940.

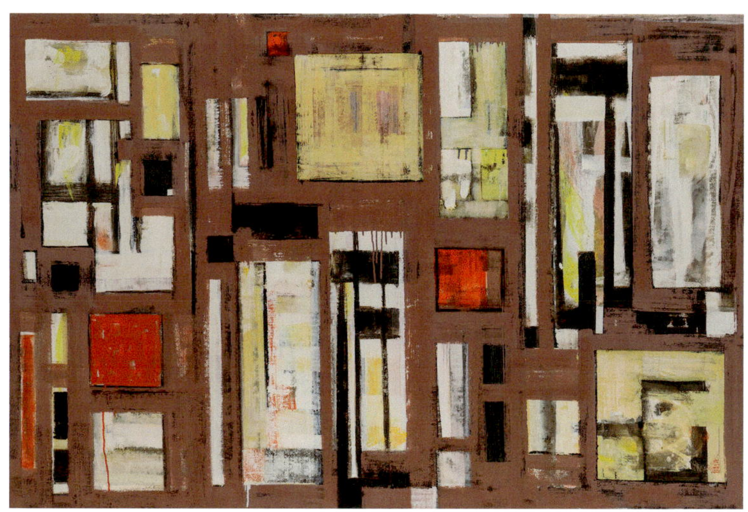

Lee Krasner, *Untitled*, 1950. Oil on canvas, 39½ × 58 in. (100.3 × 147.3 cm). Courtesy of Robert Miller Gallery, New York.

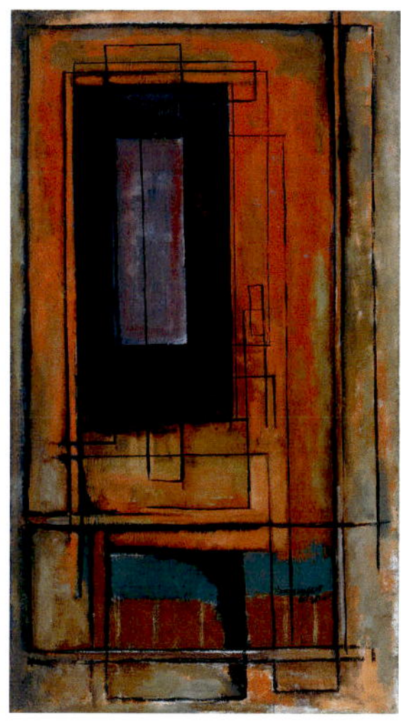

Norman Lewis, *Untitled*, 1946. Oil on canvas, 36¼ × 20⅛ in. Courtesy of Michael Rosenfeld Gallery, New York.

popular dance.[11] Later, during the 1950s, Lewis established a friendship with the painter Miró while on a tour of the Mediterranean and Spain. Krasner's paintings at the beginning of that decade reflect her interest in collage; Lewis's works suggest urban forms—specifically the architecture of Harlem, where the artist lived.

In 1945, Krasner married Jackson Pollock and the couple moved from Manhattan to Springs, East Hampton, on Long Island. During the summer of 1946 and throughout the following year, when Pollock began his drip painting, Krasner was entering a new phase in her art.[12] During this time, her works were frequently based on loose, gridded patterns, limited in color but rich in textural effects and calligraphic markings. Robert Hobbs places these works, which Krasner called Little Images, within a universal context, that of language—considered essential for civilization, the definition of the self, and as a marker of continuity—set against the tragic rupture of the Holocaust.[13]

The second half of the 1940s and the end of World War II marked major turning points for both artists. By now, Lewis's friends and associates among the abstract expressionists included Krasner and Pollock.[14] Lewis, represented by the Willard Gallery, was producing unique linear abstractions that shared much conceptually and aesthetically with the work of Reinhardt and Mark Tobey.[15] For both Krasner and Lewis, scale was in part defined by the confinement of their studio spaces. Krasner's studio was a small bedroom at Springs, and Lewis worked out of his 125th Street apartment in Harlem.[16]

In 1949, Lewis had his first solo show at Willard Gallery. Two years later, he was included in the exhibition *Abstract Painting and Sculpture in America*, organized by the Museum of Modern Art.[17] Lewis had already begun to negotiate the rationale of his approach and ambition: "The development of one's aesthetic abilities suffers by such an emphasis [on social problems]. . . . The goal of the artist must be aesthetic development and, in a universal sense, to make in his own way some contribution to culture."[18] In the spring of 1950, Lewis was the only African American artist invited to attend the private artists' symposia, organized by Franz Kline and Willem de Kooning, at Studio 35 in New York, to discuss the state of vanguard American art (see page 85).[19] The agenda ranged from art practices to mass culture, politics, and the public. Krasner's artistic activities, intellect, and ambition were apparent, but public recognition was slow in coming: her first one-person show, held at Betty Parsons Gallery in 1951, was poorly received, if not ignored.[20]

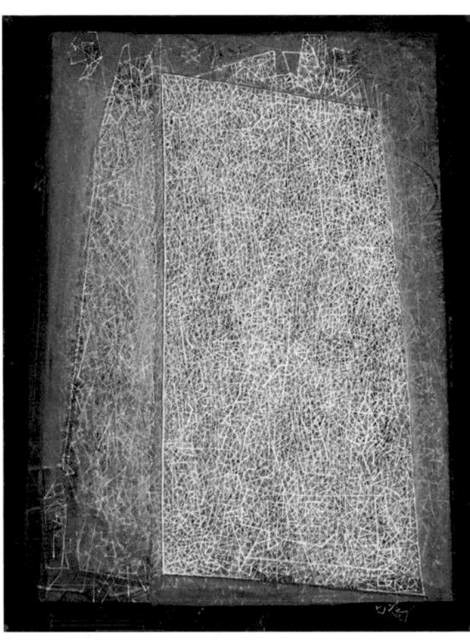

Mark Tobey, *New York Tablet*, 1946. Watercolor and chalk on paper on wood panel, 24⅞ x 19 in. (63.2 x 48.3 cm). Munson-Williams-Proctor Arts Institute, Utica, Edward W. Root Bequest.

THE LANGUAGE OF PAINTING The postwar synthesis of various artistic avenues had led Barnett Newman to prophesy, in 1944, the future of an art that was "abstract yet full of feeling," striving for a sublimity that was, somehow, beyond words.[21] The question that remained was of signification—how and with what accuracy was "feeling" being conveyed? Throughout the works of Krasner and Lewis one sees a variety of not only methods but also manners of signification: if narrative was negated by abstraction, then metaphor, metonymy, and allusion (abstract symbolism), whether through forms, titles, or associations, might still frame the reception of their works.[22]

"A painting is to be called abstract," according to Michel Seuphor, one of abstraction's committed exponents, "when it is impossible to recognize in it the slightest trace of that objective reality which makes up the normal background of our everyday experiences."[23] Abstraction has nevertheless proved as susceptible to interpretation as any other cultural object. Previously considered an arcane, even inexplicable topic by many critics as well as by artists themselves, abstract art's broad range of interpretations—whether symbolic, social, biographical, or psychoanalytic—has gained ground.[24] Although the idea of a "language" in regard to either the meanings or interpretation of abstract painting might appear contradictory, linguistic concerns enter the discussion at many levels, including the perception of a language that produces its own subject.[25] Visual "language" seen from this view performs a role related to conceptions of style—defined by Meyer Schapiro as "a system of forms with a quality and a meaningful expression through which the personality of the artist and the broad outlook of a group are visible."[26] In a further sense, visual language and its interpretation have been proposed as the actual producers of a work of art—and, by extension, of the author of that work. In the case of Krasner and Lewis, such propositions allow for an understanding of how their creations within the postwar style of abstraction might carry the possibility of a rich array of inflections—not least that of a "voice" that shifts or contradicts the ideal tendency of the given language, or style.

EVOLUTION The influence of the drip technique and gesture associated with the visual "language" of their contemporaries is clearly resonant in the work of both Krasner and Lewis. Yet the line that describes a pictorial contour moves through their work as well: in Lewis, through the creation of ciphers; in Krasner, via a type of mark making that represents the juncture of reason and the irrational.[27]

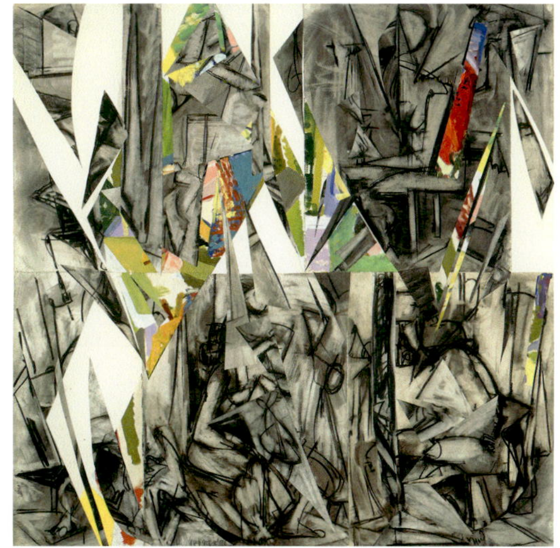

Lee Krasner, *Imperative*, 1976. Oil, charcoal, and paper on canvas, 50 × 50 in. (127 × 127 cm). National Gallery of Art, Washington, D.C., gift of Mr. and Mrs. Eugene Victor Thaw.

In *System and Dialectics of Art* (1937), John Graham considered painting as *écriture*, in the sense of a spontaneous (automatic) writing, following the concept introduced in 1924 by the surrealist André Breton. *Écriture* carries with it the connotation of a calligraphy related to gesture and has recently been adopted in reconsideration of a wide range of twentieth-century practice.[28] Emphasis is generally placed on the liberation of the unconscious mind, but there remains the implication that writing, in this visual sense, also concerns meaning, at the very least as the demonstration of an authorial self. For both artists, the appearance of painting as writing,

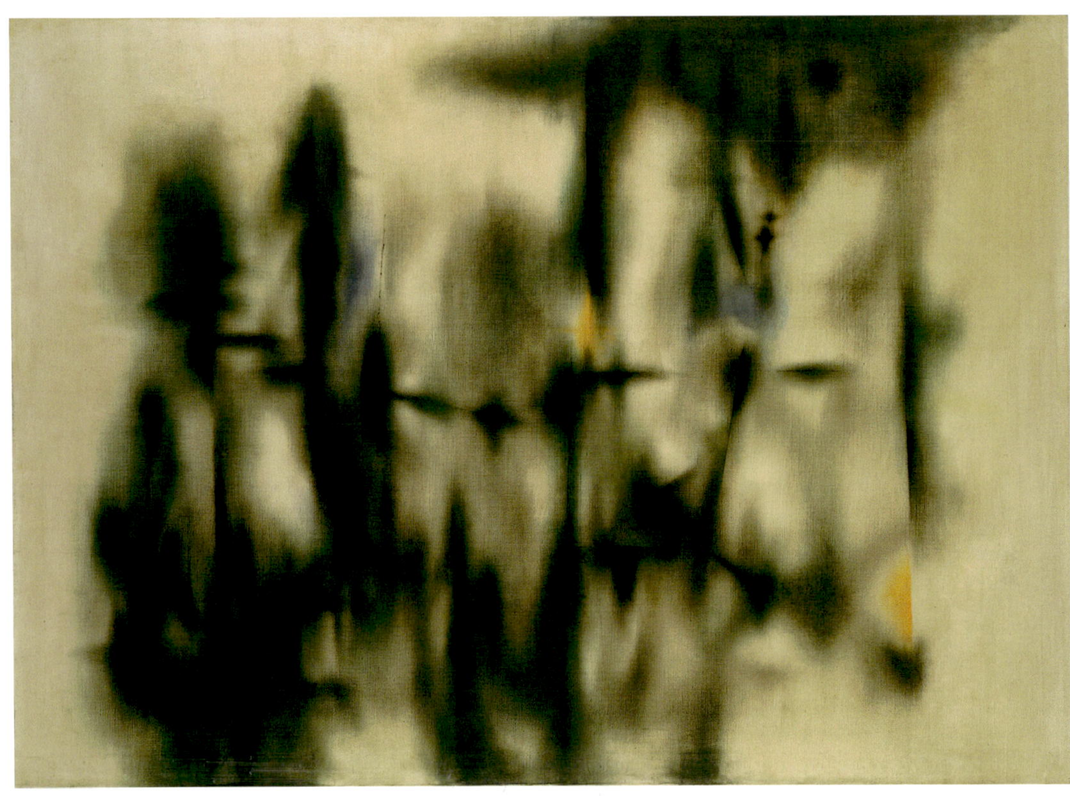

Norman Lewis, *Just Firmament*, 1951. Oil on canvas, 43 × 60 in. (109.2 × 152.4 cm).
Courtesy of Michael Rosenfeld Gallery, New York.

as *écriture*, is implicit in their investment in the pleasures and possibilities of line. Whether as record, organization (design), or fantasy, line also represents the visual means of communication par excellence, providing the potential for signification. Line, *écriture*, image, in effect suggest an order whose silent voice refers to life and social interaction.

Both artists pushed their treatment of line to extremes, in Krasner's case through the constructive cuts of the collage aesthetic versus the gestural circuits of her sumptuous celebrations of nature. By contrast, Lewis's dissolution of line, through an elegant *sfumato*, suggests a profoundly ambiguous meditation on the powers of modern science.[29] Krasner's stylistic explorations in a work such as *Kufic*, an impressive mural of 1965 (see page 65) adapts on a grand scale the possibilities of an exotic calligraphy reflective of a modernist aesthetic descended from Matisse. In a contemporaneous work such as *Processional* (see page 89) the *écriture* of Lewis extends to an engagement with the politics of the artist's time.[30]

The paintings of Lee Krasner and Norman Lewis gathered in this volume suggest several propositions regarding artistic styles and a social metaphor. Developed within a key period in American art and culture, the works offer scope for reflection on interrelated themes: art and modernity; issues of artistic expression and identity, whether of class, gender, ethnicity or race; and the relations of the mainstream and the excluded.[31] The artistic importance of the respective contributions of Krasner and Lewis remains evident. "From the margins" of the critical discourse of their time, these artists and their work present future scholars with opportunities to explore a broadening interpretive field that encompasses the individual achievements of Krasner and Lewis as well as further inquiry into abstraction and its meanings.

NOTES

1. See Norman L. Kleeblatt, "Blind Spots: Lee Krasner, Grace Hartigan, and Norman Lewis," in Norman L. Kleeblatt, ed. *Action/Abstraction: Pollock, De Kooning, and American Art, 1940–1976*, exh. cat. (New York and New Haven: Jewish Museum and Yale University Press, 2008), 145–50.

2. "I certainly was there through the formative years of abstract expressionism and I have been treated like I wasn't." Krasner's outcry against obscurity quoted in Gail Levin, *Lee Krasner: A Biography* (New York: Harper Collins [William Morrow], 2011), 419. For intimations of discrimination against Lewis, see David Anfam, "The Music of Invisibility," in Halley K. Harrisburg, ed., *Norman Lewis, Pulse: A Centennial Exhibition*, exh. cat. (New York: Michael Rosenfeld Gallery, 2009), 3–18.

3. Conventions surrounding gender and the immigrant background led to several variations on Krasner's name, which have been subject to comment or analysis by scholars: she was born Lena Krassner (October 27, 1908), self-styled variously as Lenore, "Mrs. Igor Pantuhoff," and Lee Krasner before becoming Mrs. Jackson Pollock. See "Introduction: Forming Krasner's Identity," in Ellen G. Landau, *Lee Krasner: A Catalogue Raisonné* (New York: Harry N. Abrams, 1995), 10–12; and "Krasner's Fictions," in Anne M. Wagner, *Three Artists (Three Women): Modernism and the Art of Hesse, Krasner, and O'Keeffe* (Berkeley: University of California Press, 1996), 107–8. The ultimate "fiction," for Wagner (p. 84), concerns Krasner's status as a quasi-male, i.e., as "the bearer of a fictional masculinity."

4. See the chronology established by Jeffrey D. Grove in Landau, *Lee Krasner*, 300–303.

5. For further biographical detail on Norman Wilfred Lewis (b. July 23, 1909), see Kellie Jones, "Norman Lewis Chronology," in *Norman Lewis: From the Harlem Renaissance to Abstraction* (New York: Kenkeleba House, Inc., 1989), 58–60; and Thomas Lawson, *Norman Lewis: A Retrospective* (New York: City University of New York, 1976), unpaginated.

6. Norman Lewis, "Application for Guggenheim Fellowship, 1949," in *Norman Lewis: From the Harlem Renaissance to Abstraction*, 65. Although apparently unsuccessful in his 1949 application, Lewis later received, among other awards, a 1975 Guggenheim Fellowship.

7. Krasner was introduced to John Graham (b. Ivan Gratianovitch Dombrowsky, 1886–1961) in 1941. The dates of the three MoMA shows are as follows: *Cubism and Abstract Art*, March 2–April 19, 1936; *Fantastic Art, Dada, Surrealism*, December 7, 1936–January 17, 1937; *African Negro Art*, March 18–May 1935. For more on the breadth of the influence of Picasso's achievement, see Michael C[owan] FitzGerald, *Picasso and American Art*, exh. cat. (New Haven: Yale University Press, 2007). Lewis's library contained copies of Barr's books and catalogues on Picasso (1939), Feininger and Hartley (1945), and Klee (1945).

See the list prepared by Joan Murray Weissman in *Norman Lewis, From the Harlem Renaissance to Abstraction*, 67–70. Picasso and José Clemente Orozco were the only modern artists reproduced in Graham's admittedly idiosyncratic volume *System and Dialectics of Art* (New York: Delphic Studios, 1937). For the emerging American vanguard, Graham's writings seemed revelatory. See Norman L. Kleeblatt, "An Expressionist in New York: Soutine's Reception in America at Mid-Century," in Norman L. Kleeblatt and Kenneth E. Silver, *An Expressionist in Paris: The Paintings of Chaim Soutine* (Munich and New York: Prestel and the Jewish Museum, 1998), 50–51 ("Soutine Theorized: John Graham's Historical Trajectory").

8. Founded in New York in 1936, the association continues its activities today.

9. See Ann Eden Gibson, "Black Is a Color: Norman Lewis and Modernism in New York," in *Norman Lewis: Black Paintings, 1946–1977*, exh. cat. (New York: Studio Museum in Harlem, 1998), 15. The school was founded by the Communist party in 1944 and shut down in 1956.

10. Ad Reinhardt, *How to Look at Modern Art in America*, published in *P.M.*, June 2, 1946. A related drawing appeared as *The Imaginary Museum*, in *Art d'aujourd'hui*, June 1951. Krassner [*sic*] and Lewis appear as leaves in both. A bilious reprise of the first appeared under the same title in *Art News*, summer 1961. See Robert Storr, *How to Look. Ad Reinhardt Art Comics* (New York and Ostfildern: David Zwirner and Hatje Cantz, 2013), 34–35, 76–77, 88–89, ills.

11. For Krasner's personal encounter with Mondrian (1872–1944), see Levin, *Lee Krasner* (2011), esp. 180–82. On Mondrian and dance, see Annette Chauncy, "Dancing with Mondrian," *International Journal of the Arts in Society* 5, no. 3 (2010): 181–91.

12. The relation of Krasner's work with that of Pollock was the subject of an exhibition titled *Artists: Man and Wife*, organized in 1949 at the gallery of Sidney Janis in New York, followed in 1981 by *Krasner-Pollock: A Working Relationship*, organized by Barbara Rose for the Grey Art Gallery at New York University. The Krasner-Pollock relationship has continued to provide an armature for (varying) interpretations. See Ralf Leisner, *Lee Krasner–Jackson Pollock: eine Ateliergemeinschaft, 1942–1956* (Munich: Scaneg, 1995); and Wagner, "Krasner's Fictions."

13. See Robert Hobbs, *Lee Krasner*, exh. cat. (New York: Independent Curators International, in association with Harry N. Abrams, 1999), 64–92. Regarding Krasner's interest in script and "exotic writing," see Levin, *Lee Krasner*, 369–70. Myriad listings of sources and influences on Krasner's Little Images occur in Landau, *Lee Krasner*, 100–117.

14. For indication of Lewis's contact with other abstract expressionists, see Gibson, "Black Is a Color," 28 n30.

15. The wake for Reinhardt, who was a friend to both Lewis and Krasner, was held by Krasner in her home at Springs. See Levin, *Lee Krasner*, 381.

16. See Landau, *Lee Krasner*, 104, who suggests that experimental doubt also played a role in the small scale of Krasner's work of this period. Compare also Wagner, "Krasner's Fictions," esp. 142–49.

17. The exhibition ran from January 23 through March 25, 1951, and included Lewis's *Urban*, 1950 (oil on canvas, 50 × 29¾ in. [127 × 75.57 cm]). The frontispiece of the catalogue reproduces Mark Tobey's *Tundra*, 1944; both artists were represented by the Willard Gallery at the time. See Andrew Carnduff Ritchie, *Abstract Painting and Sculpture in America*, exh. cat. (New York: Museum of Modern Art, 1951), 100, ill.

18. Lewis, "Application for Guggenheim Fellowship."

19. Transcripts of the meetings, held April 21–23, 1950, were edited by the artist Robert Goodnough. See *Artists' Sessions at Studio 35* (Chicago: Soberscove Press, 2009, reprint).

20. See Kleeblatt, "Blind Spots," 147. After one-person shows at the Betty Parsons and Martha Jackson galleries (1951 and 1958, respectively), Krasner mounted periodic solo exhibitions throughout the 1960s, leading up to important exhibitions held in 1973 at Marlborough Gallery (*Recent Paintings*) and the Whitney Museum of American Art (*Large Paintings*) in New York.

21. "Sobre el arte moderno: examen y ratificación," in *La Rivista Belga* (November 1944). See John P. O'Neill, ed., *Barnett Newman, Selected Writings and Interviews* (Berkeley and Los Angeles: University of California Press, 1990), 69.

22. A hermeneutics of abstraction is proposed in Briony Fer, *On Abstract Art* (New Haven: Yale University Press, 1997), 4; and Mark Godfrey, *Abstraction and the Holocaust* (New Haven: Yale University Press, 2007), 5. See also Kobena Mercer,

ed., *Discrepant Abstraction*, Annotating Art's Histories 2 (London and Cambridge, Mass.: Institute of International Visual Arts and MIT, 2006); and Paul Crowther and Isabel Wünsche, eds., *Meanings of Abstract Art: Between Nature and Theory*, Routledge Advances in Art and Visual Studies 2 (New York and London: Routledge, 2012).

23. Michel Seuphor, *A Dictionary of Abstract Painting: Preceded by a History of Abstract Painting* (London: Methuen, 1957), 3.

24. In analyzing the case of the Armenian immigrant Arshile Gorky, for example, the idea of the appropriation of artistic language or, rather, languages, is implicit throughout Harold Rosenberg's characterization. Vosdanig Manoug Adoian, in this reading, is the immigrant for whom parody, quotation, and impersonation from the "alphabet" established by other artists are key to the outstanding question of identity. See Harold Rosenberg, *Arshile Gorky: The Man, The Time, The Idea* (New York: Horizon, 1962), esp. 36–65.

25. The attempt to constrain aesthetic discourse at mid-century has understandably attracted scholarly attention. See Ann Eden Gibson, "The Rhetoric of Abstract Expressionism," in Michael Auping, ed., *Abstract Expressionism: The Critical Developments* (New York and Buffalo: Harry N. Abrams, in association with Albright-Knox Art Gallery, 1987), 64–93; Peter J[ohannes] Schneemann, *Who's Afraid of the Word? Die Strategie der Texte bei Barnett Newman und seinen Zeitgenossen*, Rombach Wissenschaft, Reihe Quellen zur Kunst 6 (Freiburg im Breisgau: Rombach, 1998); and Schneemann, *Von der Apologie zur Theoriebildung: die Geschichtsschreibung des Abstrakten Expressionismus* Acta humaniora (Berlin: Akademie Verlag, 2003).

26. Meyer Schapiro, "Style," in Alfred Louis Kroeber, ed., *Anthropology Today* (Chicago: University of Chicago Press, 1953), 287. Compare the position of Roland Barthes in "The Death of the Author," no. 5 (Manteia, 1968).

27. Krasner's works from 1946 to 1949 have been cited as indicative of "the classic feminine condition" and as "rationalisms with nothing to say," reflecting inarticulate deference to Pollock's mastery. See Wagner, "Krasner's Fictions," esp. 142–46. In Lewis's case, there is the suggestion of the artist's "conscious stylization"—a manner that was out of step with contemporary notions of the autonomy of pure painting. See Gibson, "Norman Lewis in the Forties," in *Norman Lewis: From the Harlem Renaissance to Abstraction*, 18.

28. Graham, *System and Dialectics of Art*. See also Peter Fischer, "Abstraction, Gesture, *Écriture*, An Introduction," in *Abstraction, Gesture, Écriture: Paintings from the Daros Collection* (Zurich and Berlin/New York: Alesco/Scalo, 1999), esp. 19–20; and Crowther and Wünsche, eds., *Meanings of Abstract Art*,, esp. the contributions by Elizabeth Langhorne and Birgit Mersmann on *écriture* in Pollock and in the work of Henri Michaux, respectively. For Graham and Krasner, see Levin, *Lee Krasner*, 186.

29. On Lewis's doubt regarding modern science, see Gibson, "Black Is a Color," 19–20.

30. Although skeptical of the power of social realism, Lewis remained active in the struggle for civil rights throughout his life. See Gibson, "Black Is a Color."

31. Identity issues for both artists are treated by Ann Eden Gibson in *Abstract Expressionism, Other Politics* (New Haven: Yale University Press, 1997) and Joan Marter, ed., *Abstract Expressionism: The International Context* (New Brunswick, N.J.: Rutgers University Press, 2007).

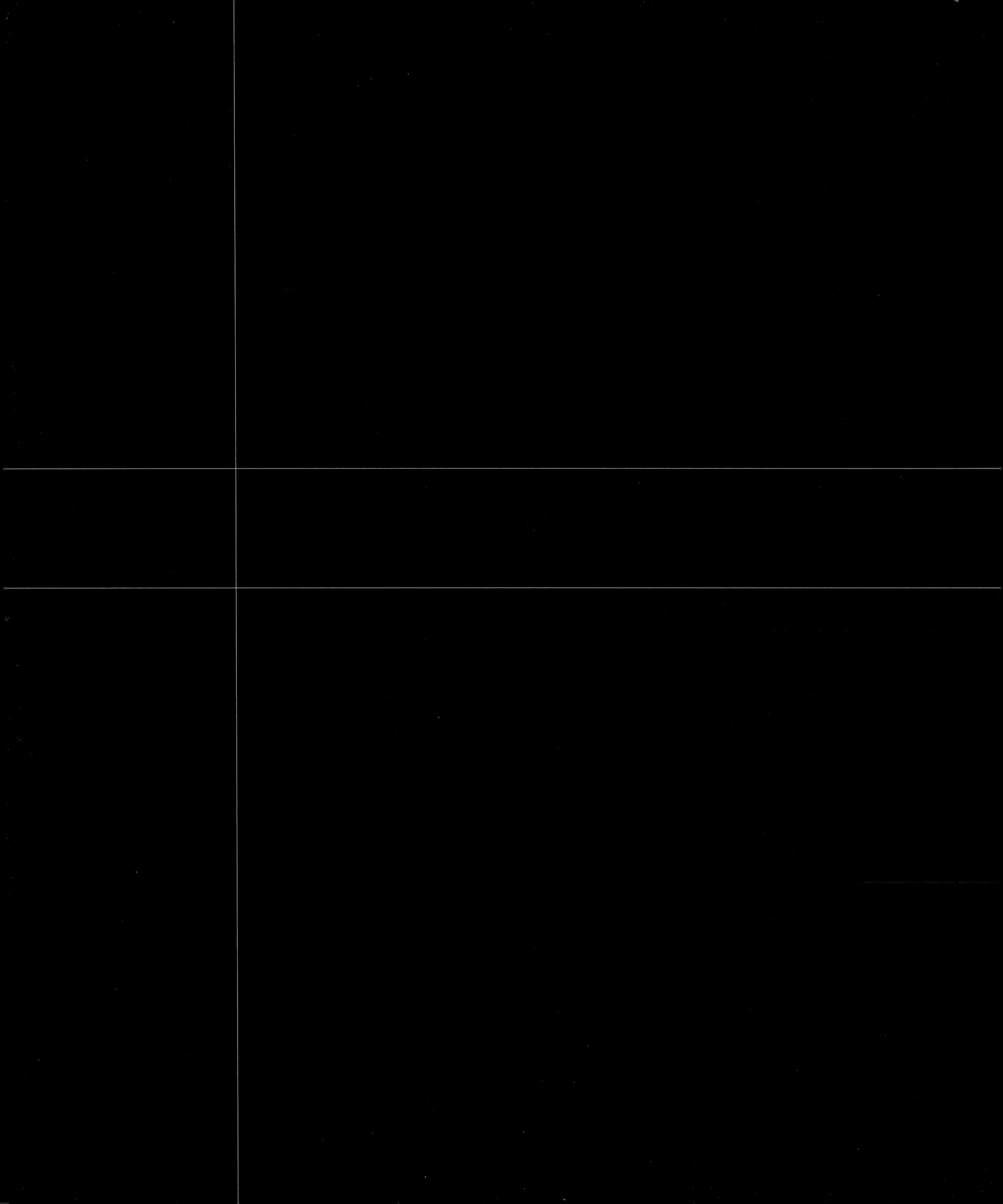

LEE KRASNER | NORMAN LEWIS

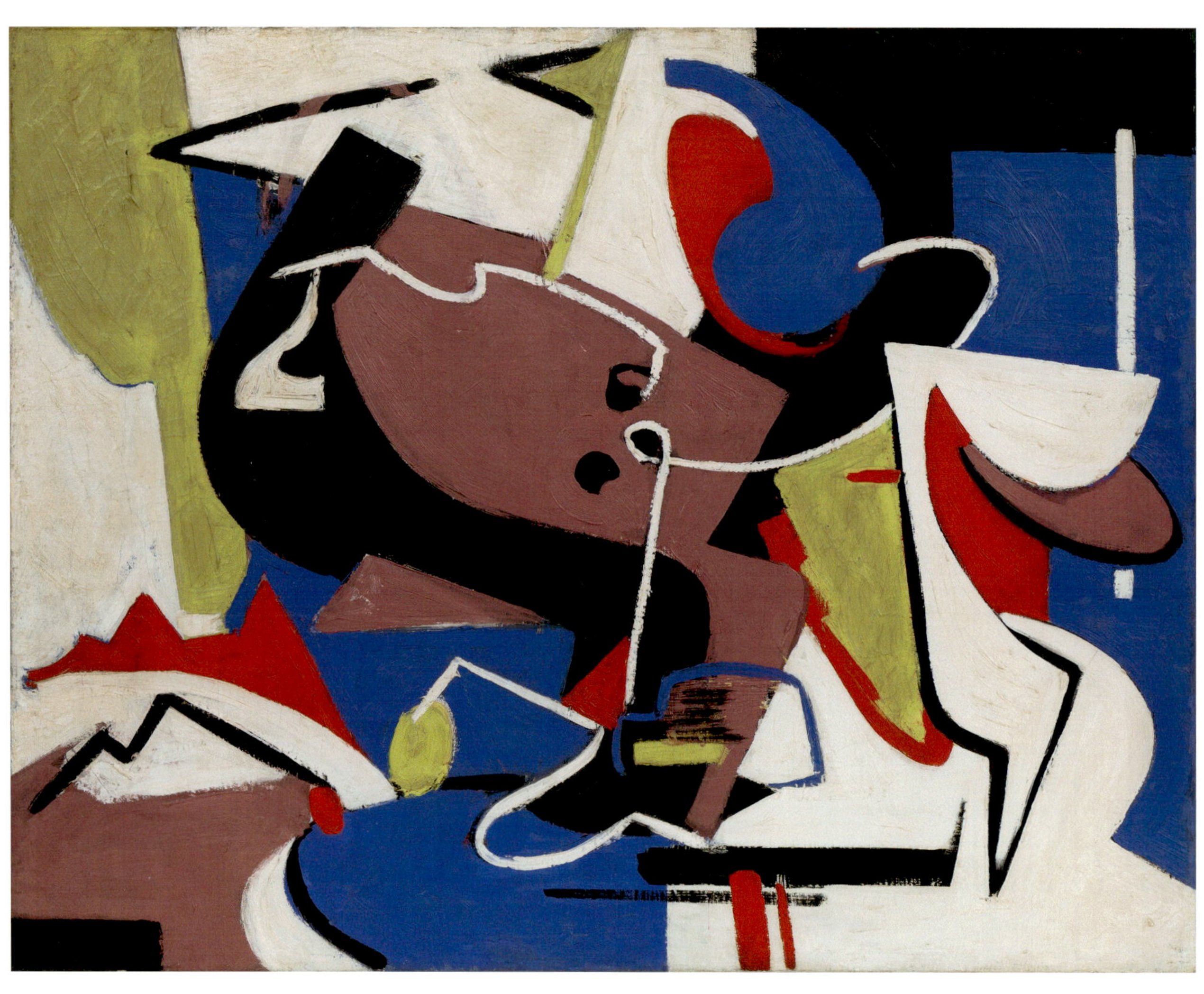

LEE KRASNER, *Lavender*, 1942. Oil on canvas, 24 × 30 in. (61 × 76.2 cm).
Courtesy of Robert Miller Gallery, New York.

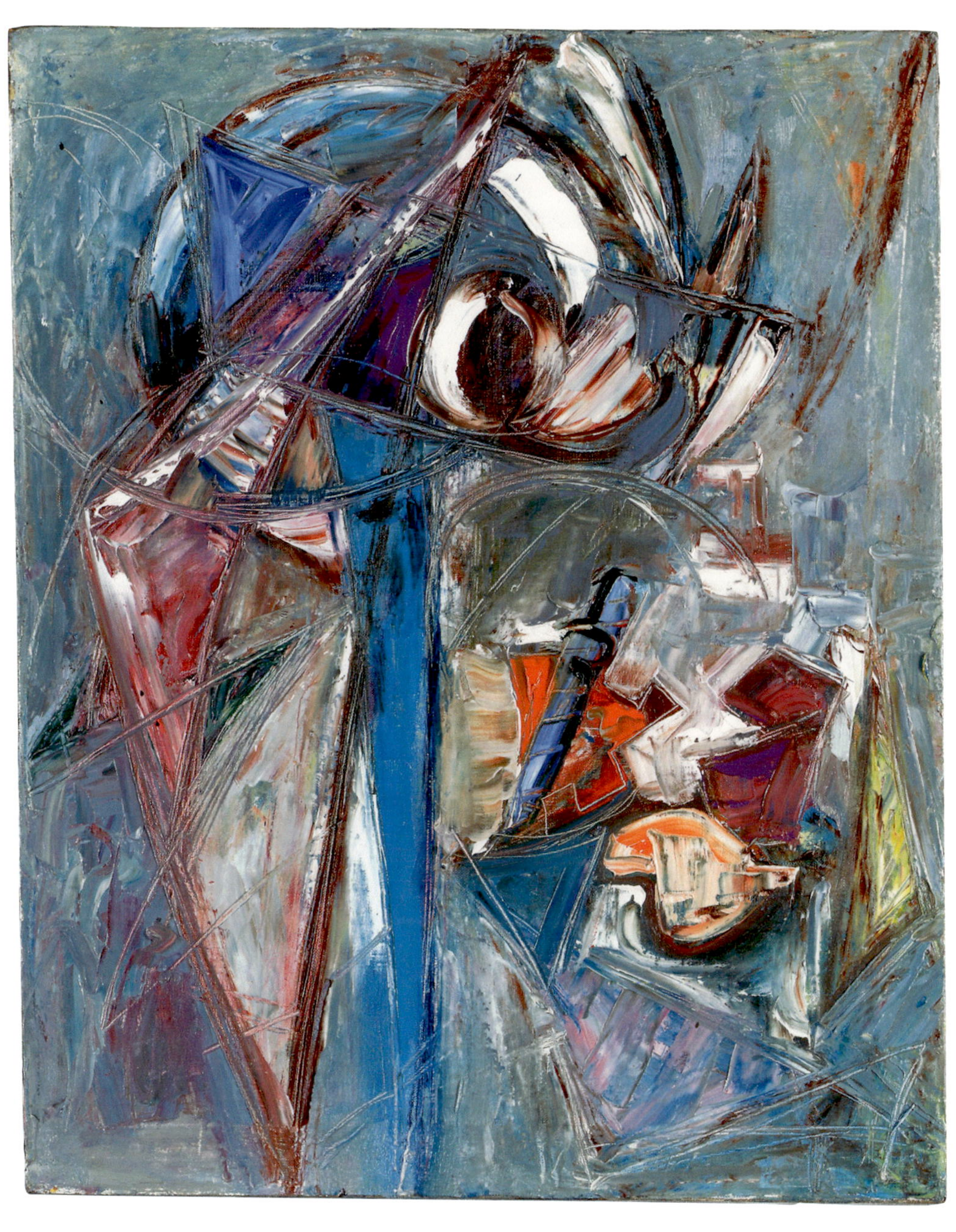

LEE KRASNER, *Image Surfacing*, c. 1945. Oil on canvas, 27 × 21¼ in. (68.6 x 51.4 cm).
Private collection.

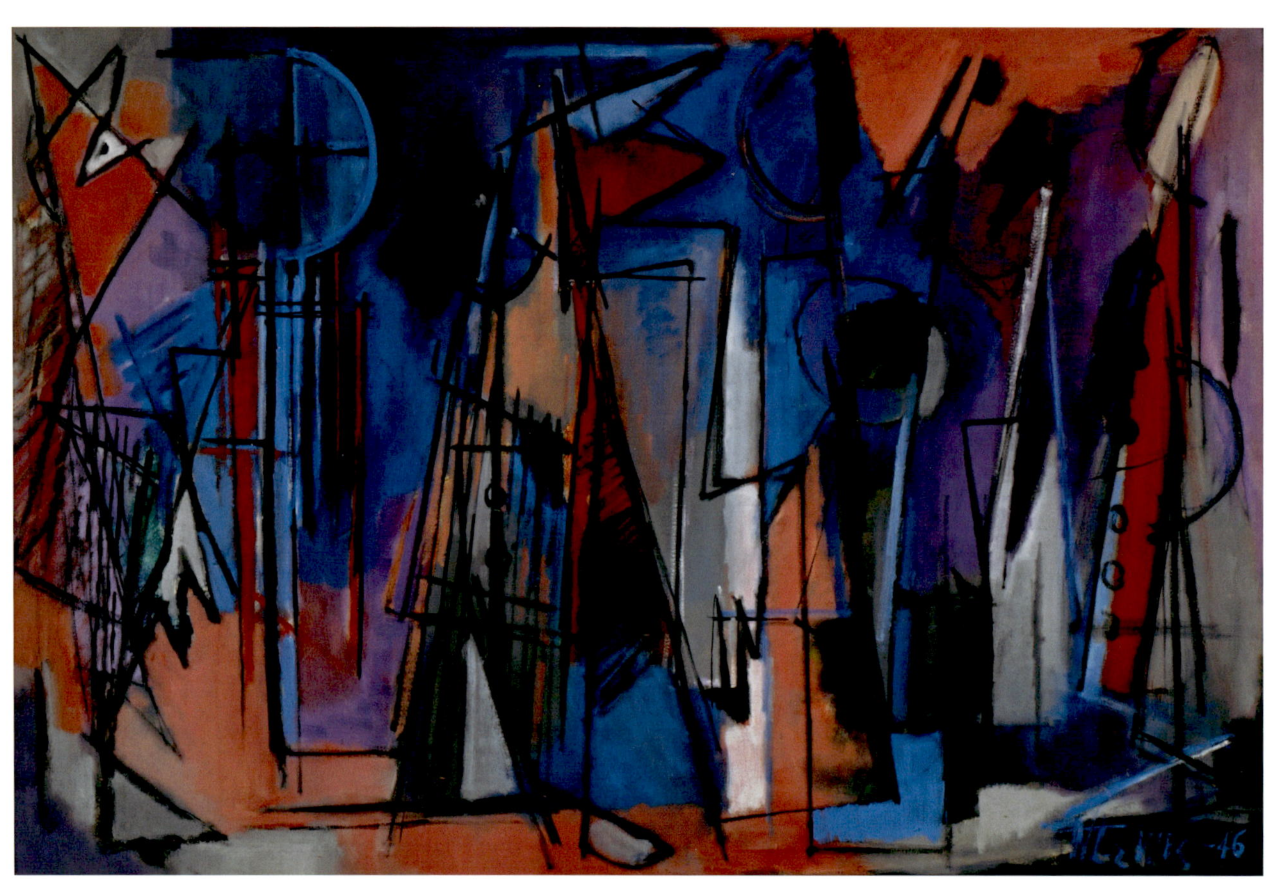

NORMAN LEWIS, *Untitled*, 1946. Oil on canvas, 32¾ × 48 in. (83.2 × 121.9 cm).
Studio Museum in Harlem, Bequest of Irene Wheeler.

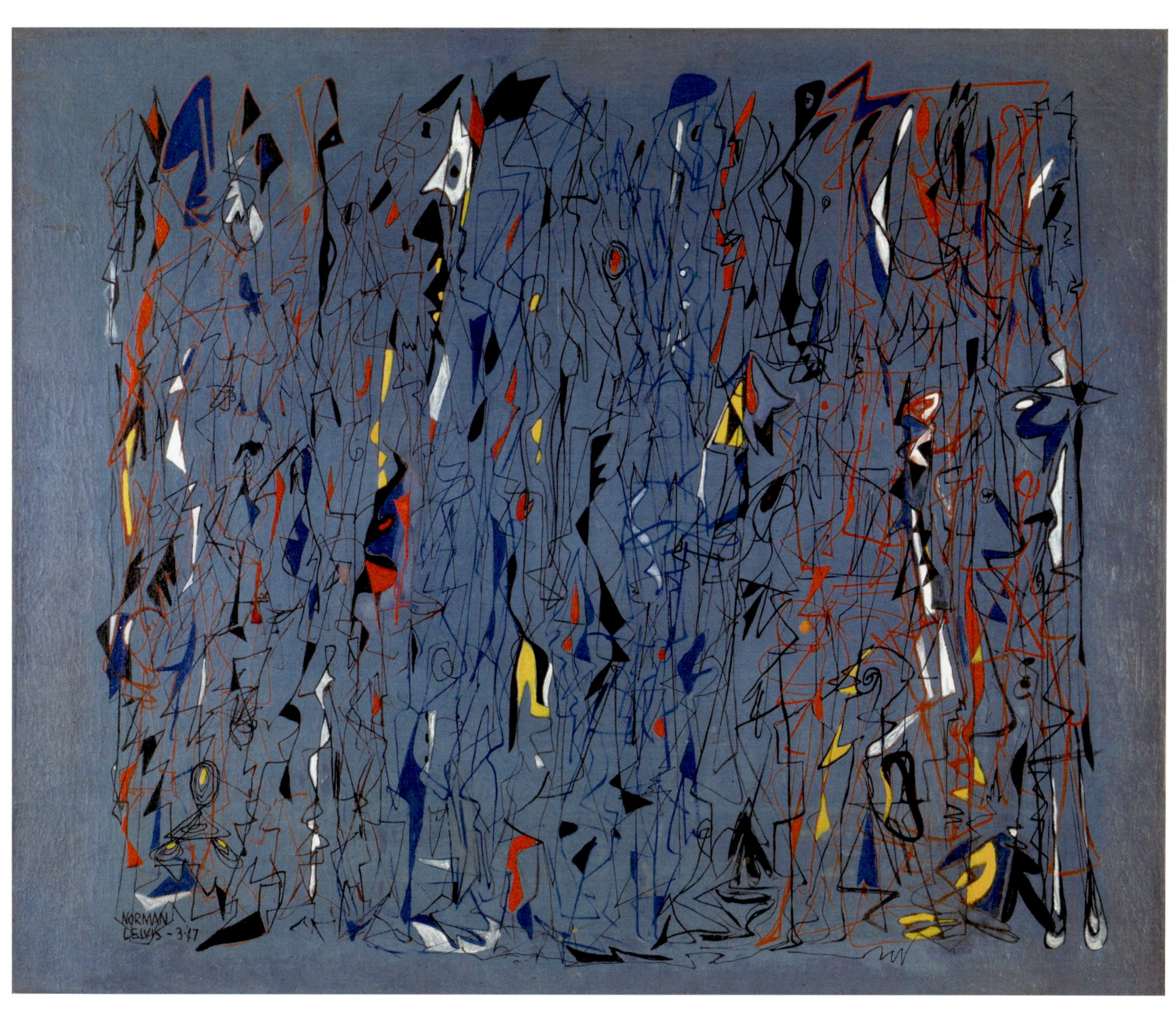

NORMAN LEWIS, *Twilight Sounds*, 1947. Oil on canvas, 23½ × 28 in. (59.7 x 71.1 cm). Saint Louis Art Museum, Missouri, Funds given by Mr. and Mrs. John Peters MacCarthy, Mr. and Mrs. Harvey Saligman, Billy E. Hodges, and the Art Endowment Fund.

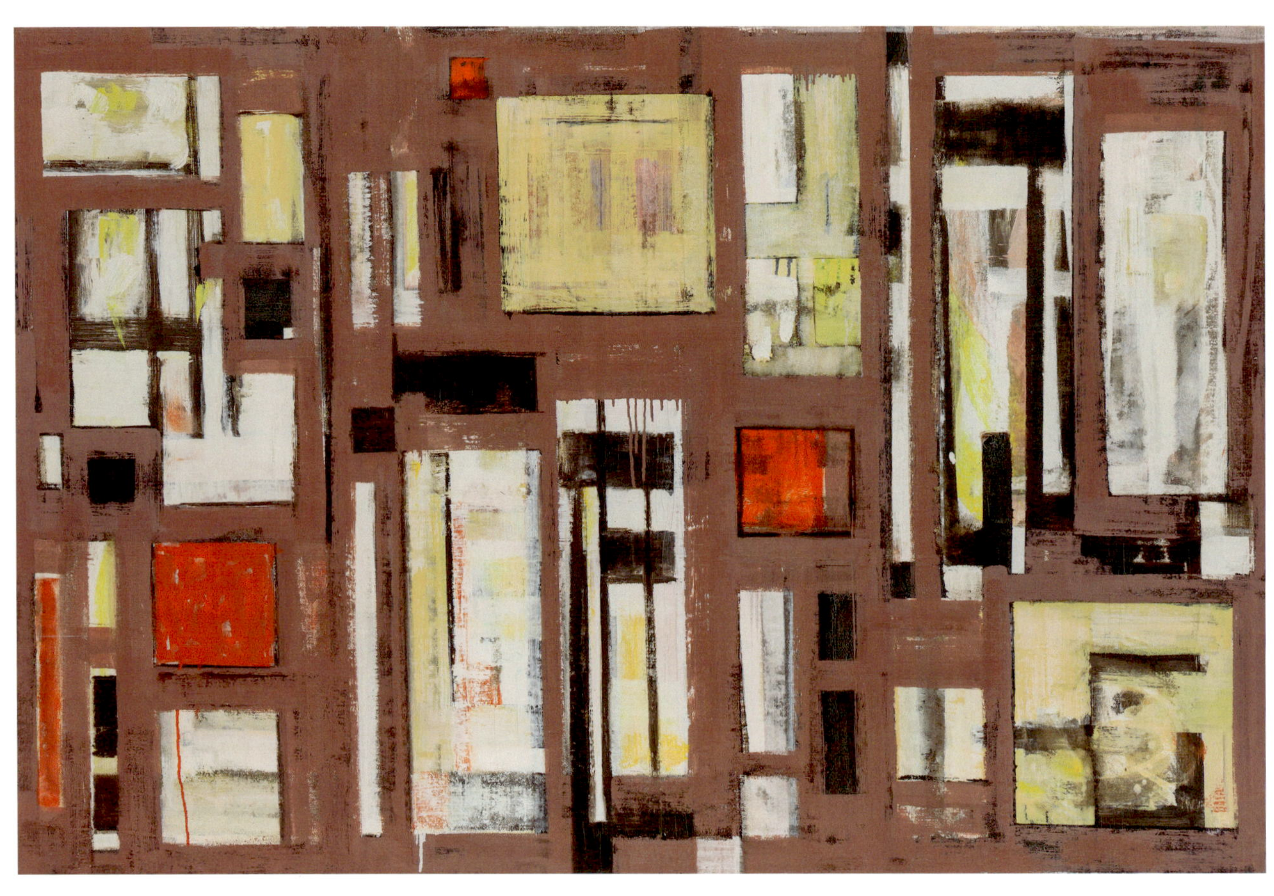

LEE KRASNER, *Untitled*, 1950. Oil on canvas, 39½ × 58 in. (100.3 × 147.3 cm).
Courtesy of Robert Miller Gallery, New York.

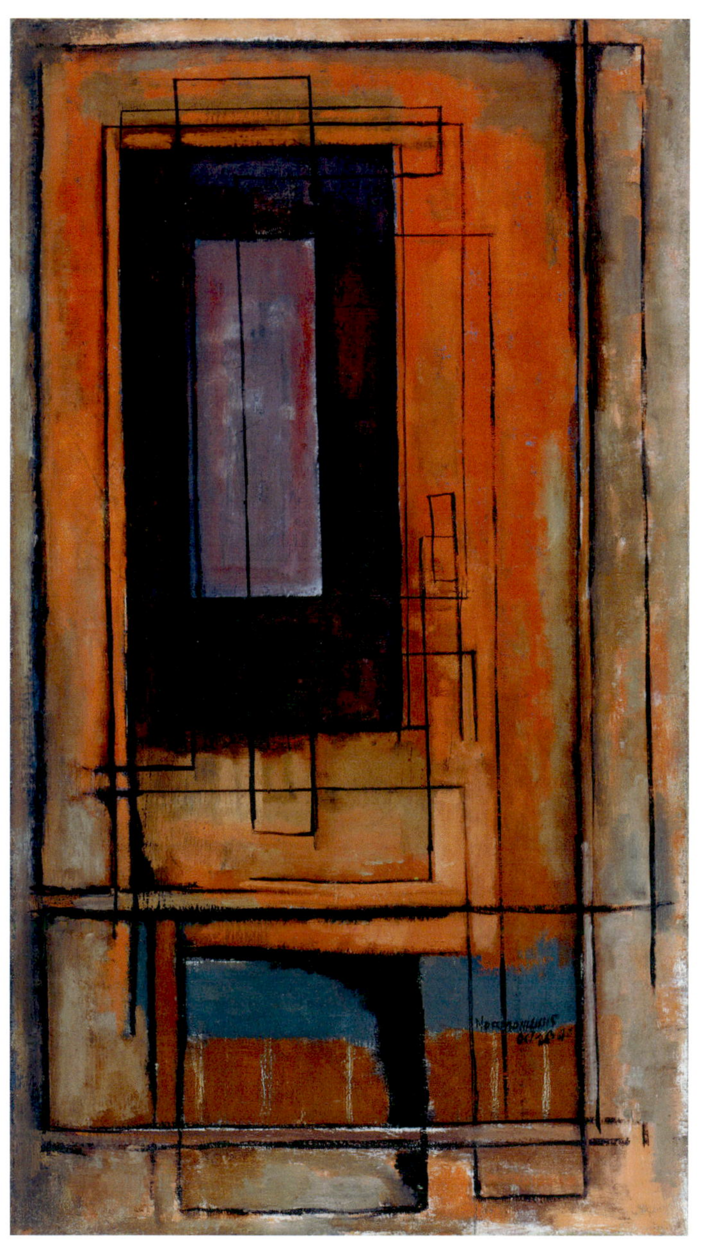

NORMAN LEWIS, *Untitled*, 1946. Oil on canvas, 36¼ × 20⅛ in. (92.1 × 51.1 cm).
Courtesy of Michael Rosenfeld Gallery, New York.

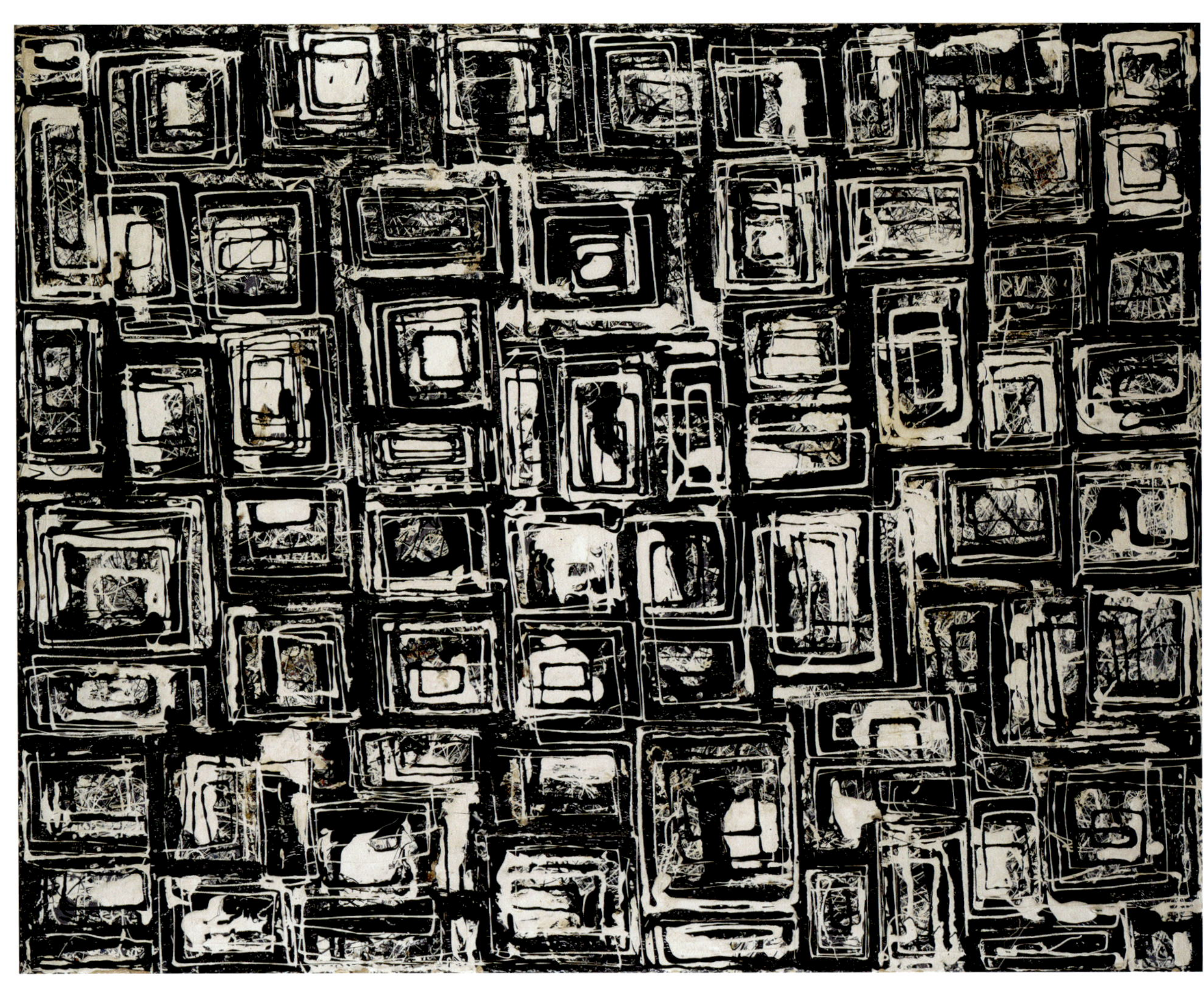

LEE KRASNER, *Black and White Squares No. 1*, 1948. Oil and enamel on linen, 24 × 30 in. (61 × 76.2 cm). Private collection, courtesy of Matthew Marks Gallery, New York.

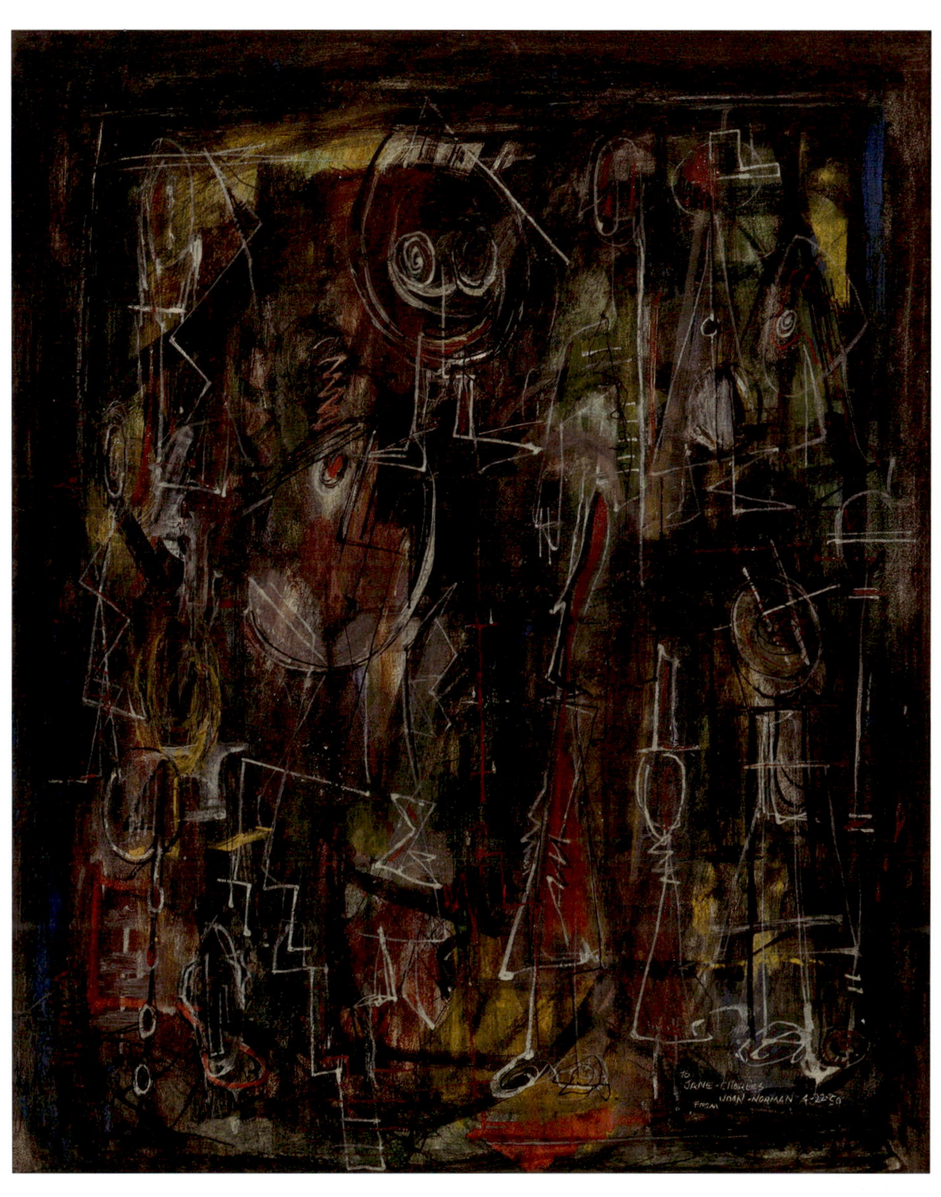

NORMAN LEWIS, *Untitled*, c. 1946–48. Oil on masonite, 20 × 15½ in. (50.8 × 39.4 cm).
Collection of Raymond J. McGuire.

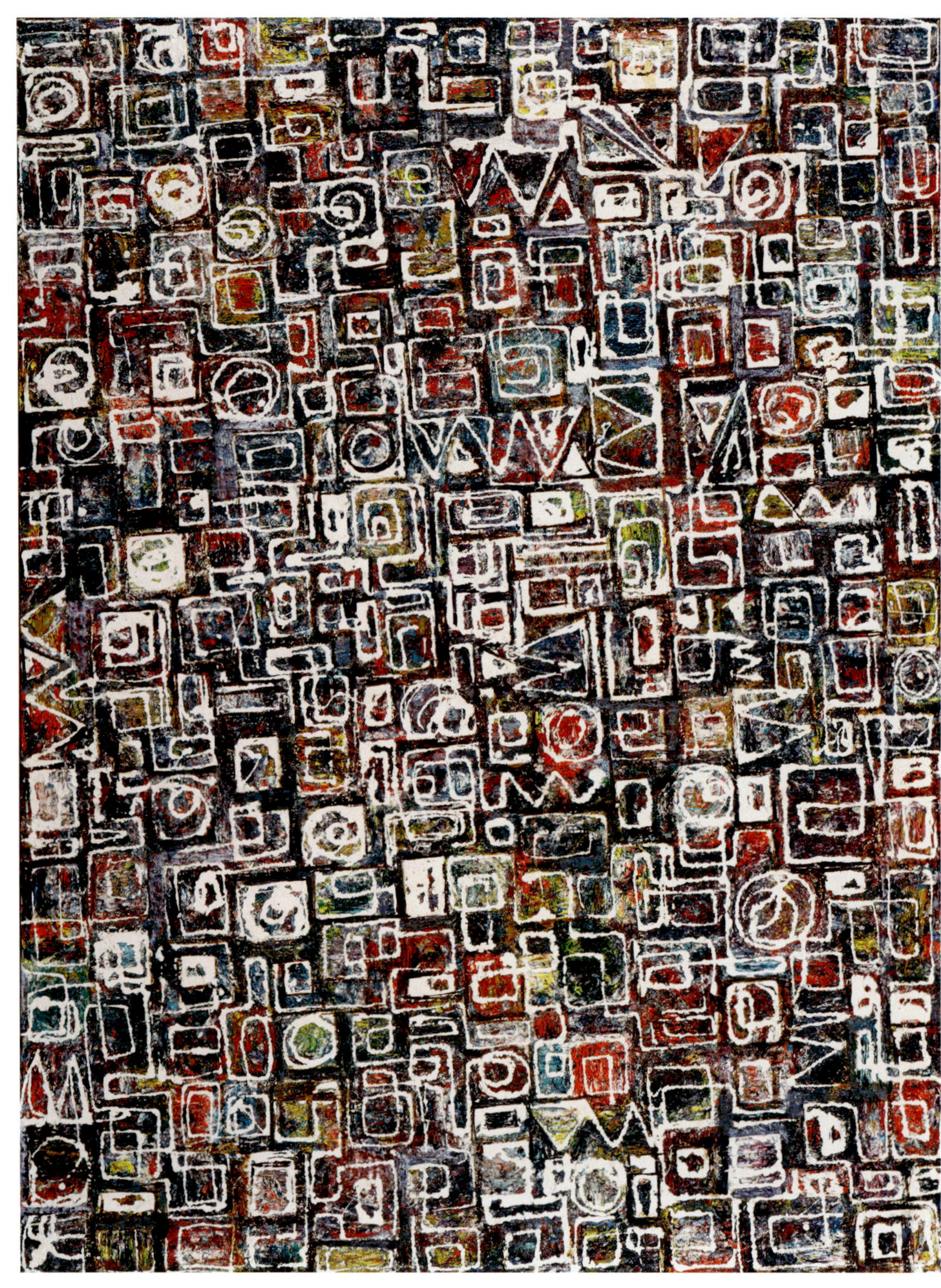

LEE KRASNER, *Composition*, 1949. Oil on canvas, 38 × 28 in. (96.5 × 71.1 cm).
Philadelphia Museum of Art, Gift of The Aaron E. Norman Fund, Inc., 1959.

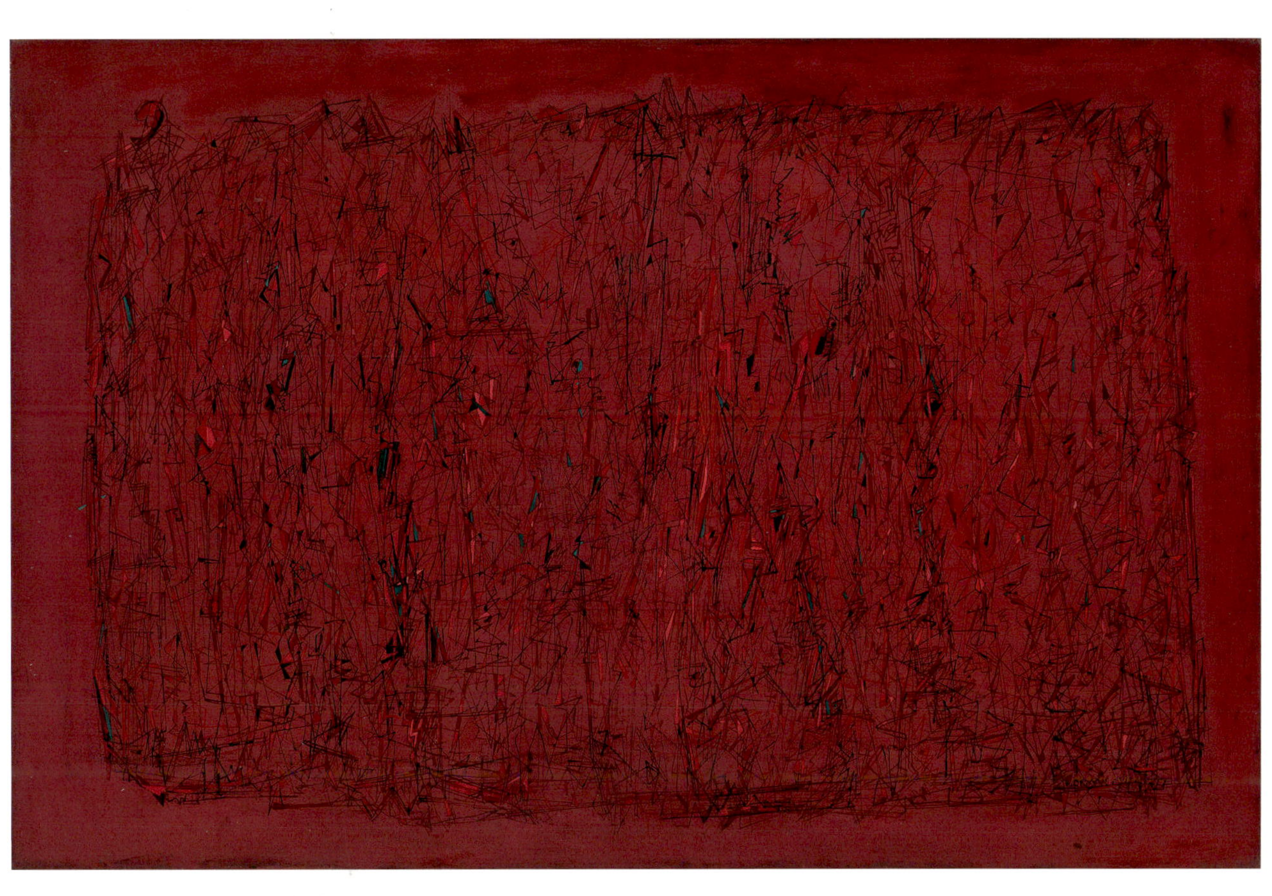

NORMAN LEWIS, *Magenta Haze*, 1947. Oil on canvas, 24 × 36 in. (61 × 91.4 cm).
Courtesy of Michael Rosenfeld Gallery, New York.

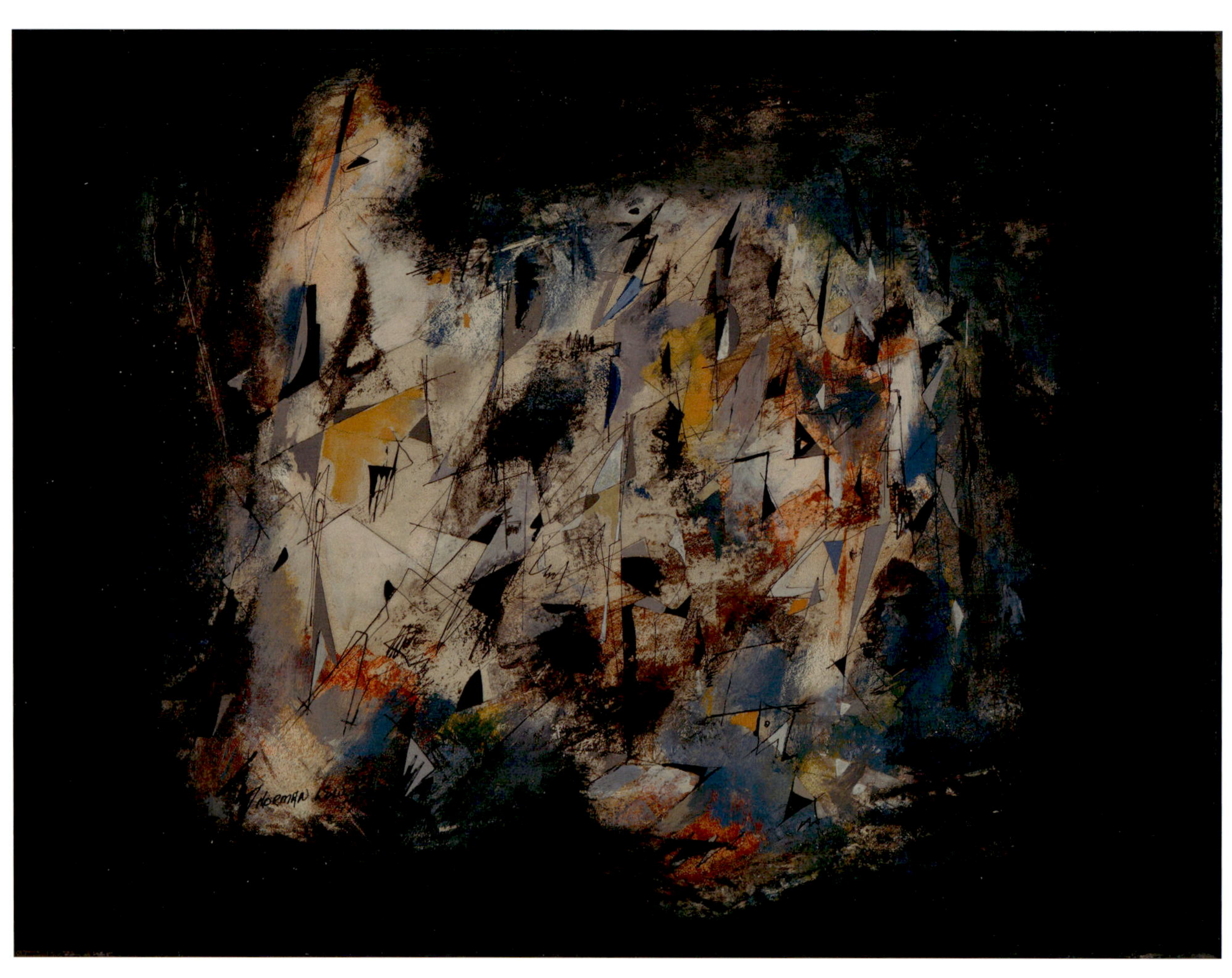

NORMAN LEWIS, *Florence*, 1947. Oil on masonite, 14 × 18 in. (35.6 × 45.7 cm).
Elisha Hawkins Collection of African American and African Art.

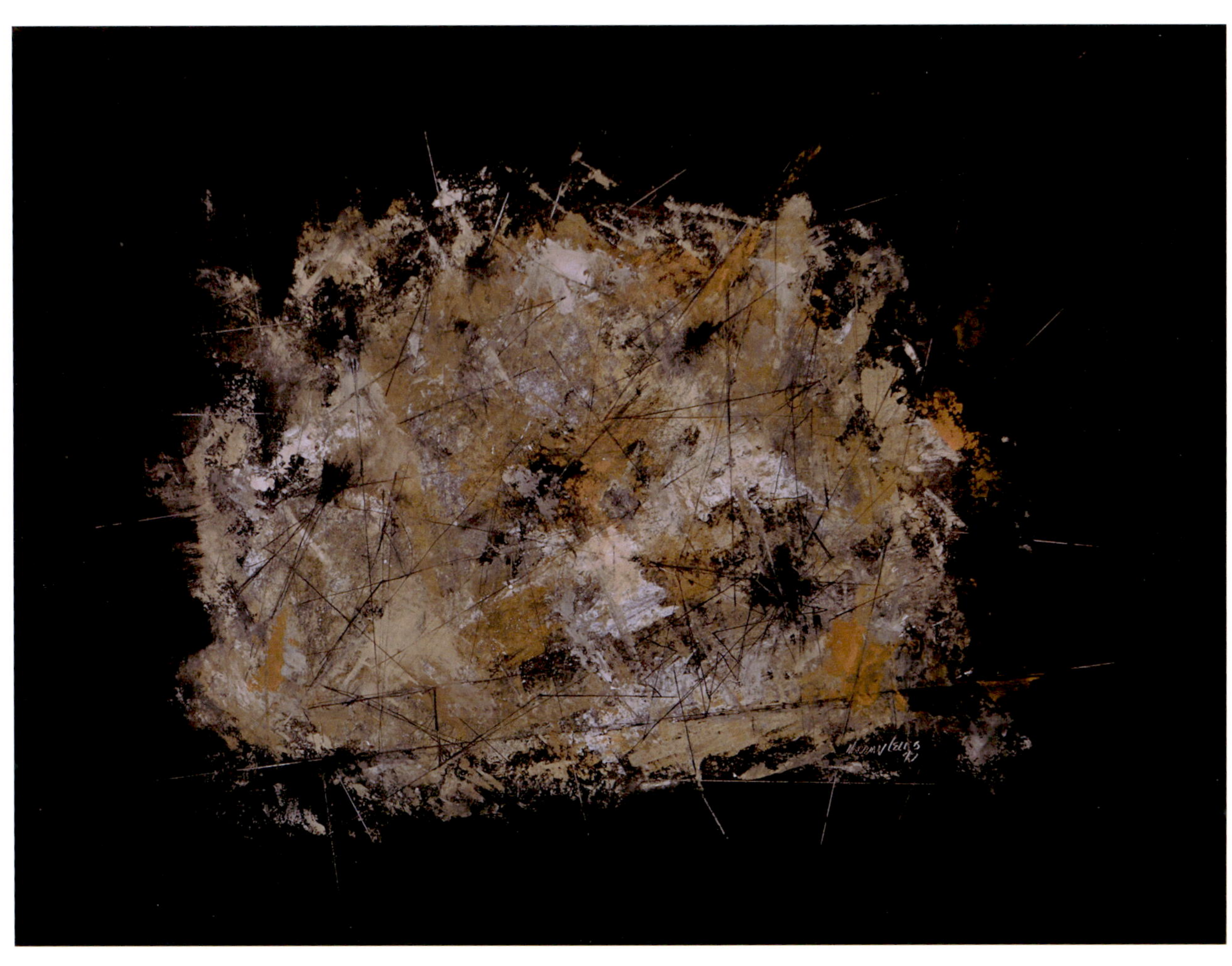

NORMAN LEWIS, *Shapes*, 1947. Oil on masonite, 14½ × 17¾ in. (36.8 × 45 cm).
Collection of Betty A. Davis, New York.

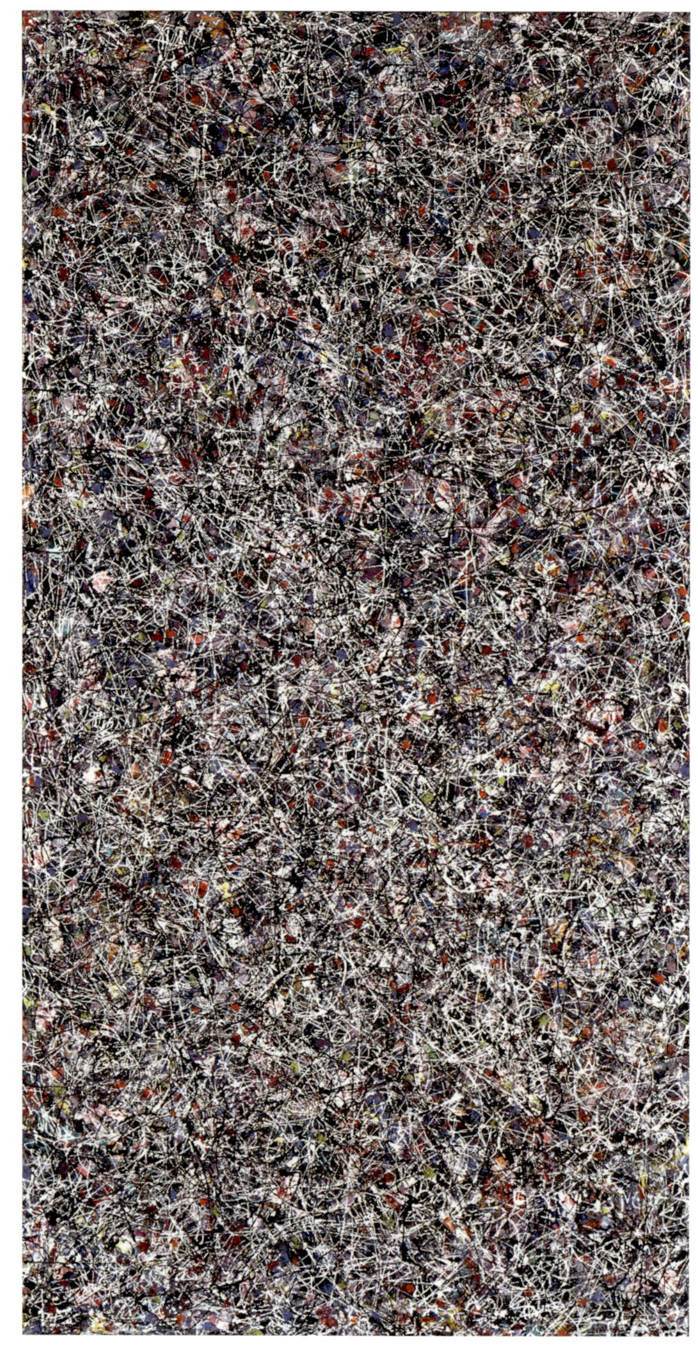

LEE KRASNER, *Untitled*, 1948–49. Oil on canvas, 42⅛ × 21⅛ in. (106.9 x 53.7 cm).
Collection of halley k harrisburg and Michael Rosenfeld, New York.

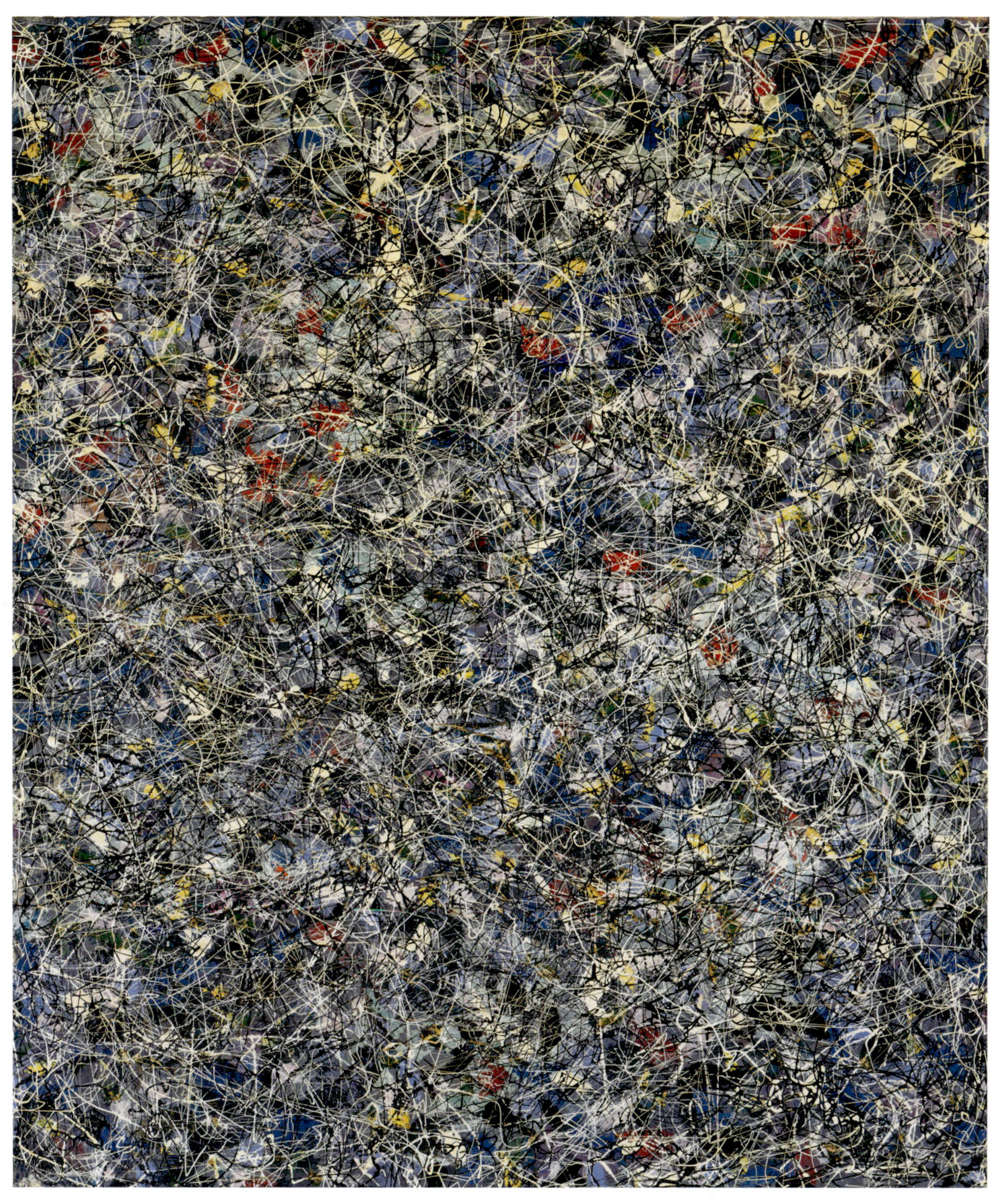

LEE KRASNER, *Untitled*, 1948. Oil on canvas, 30 × 25 in. (76.2 × 63.5 cm).
The Metropolitan Museum of Art, New York, Gift of Mrs. Donald T. Braider, 1986.

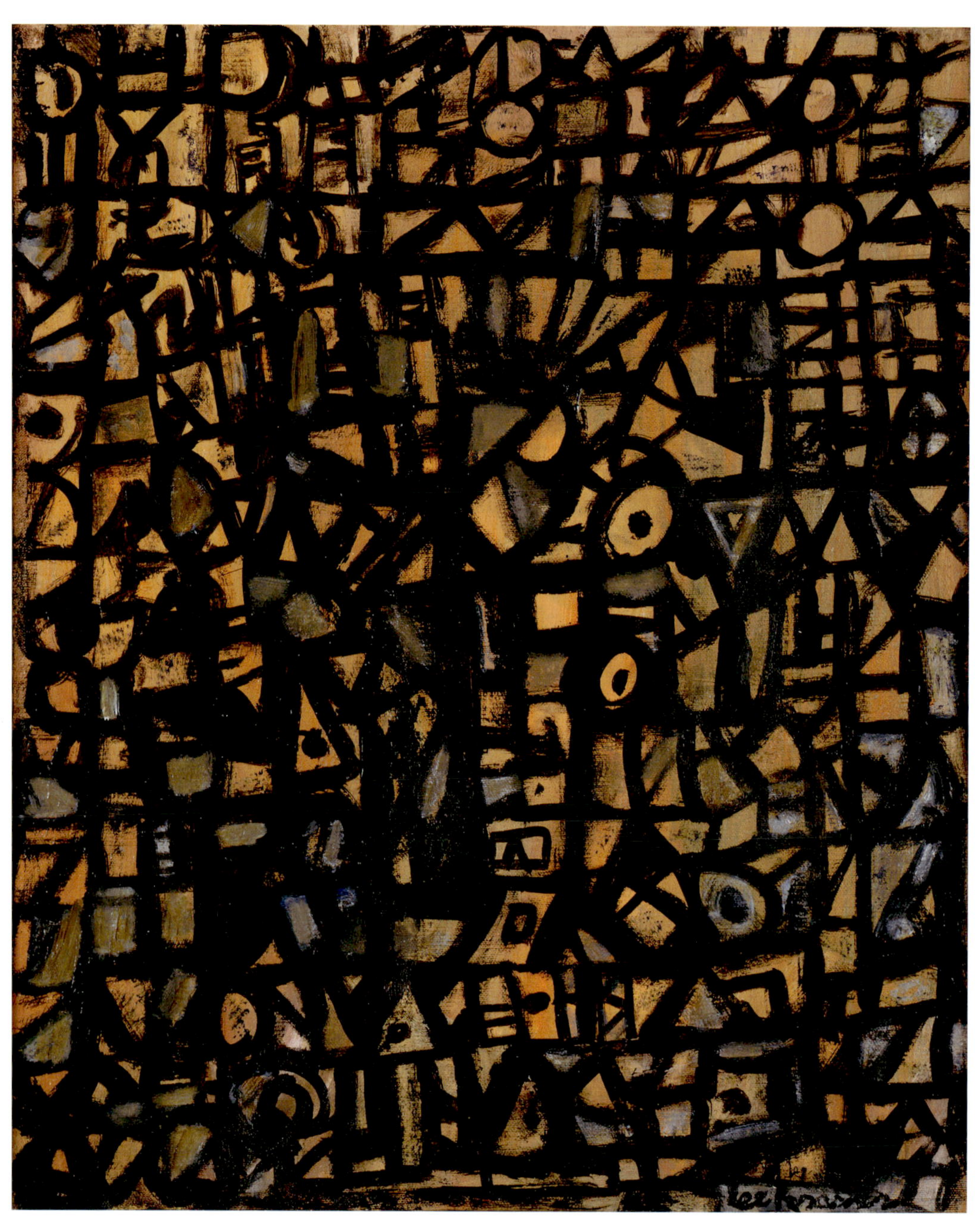

LEE KRASNER, *Untitled,* 1949. Oil on canvas, 20 × 16 in. (50.8 × 40.6 cm).
Courtesy of Michael Rosenfeld Gallery, New York.

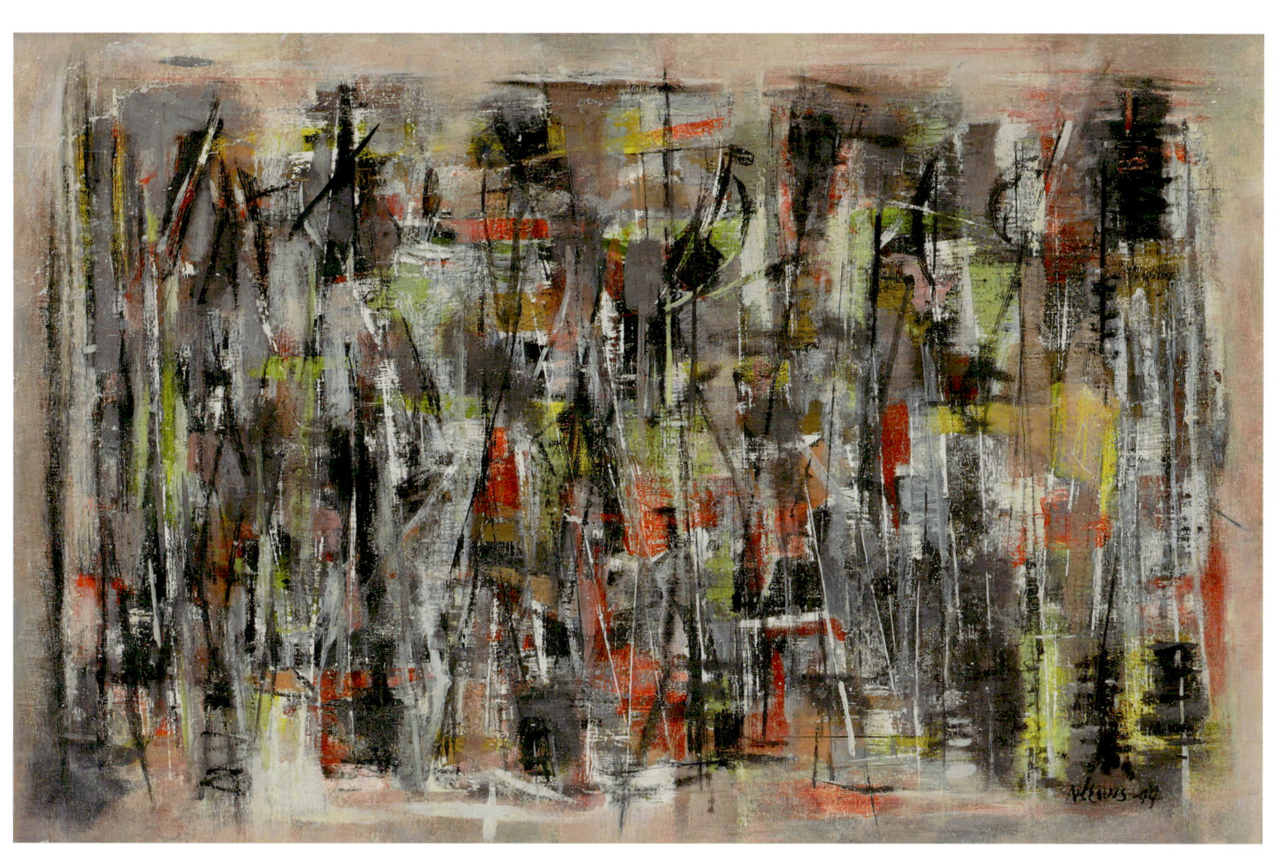

NORMAN LEWIS, *Untitled,* 1949. Oil on canvas, 20 × 30 in. (50.8 × 76.2 cm).
Collection of Pamela J. Joyner/Alfred J. Giuffrida.

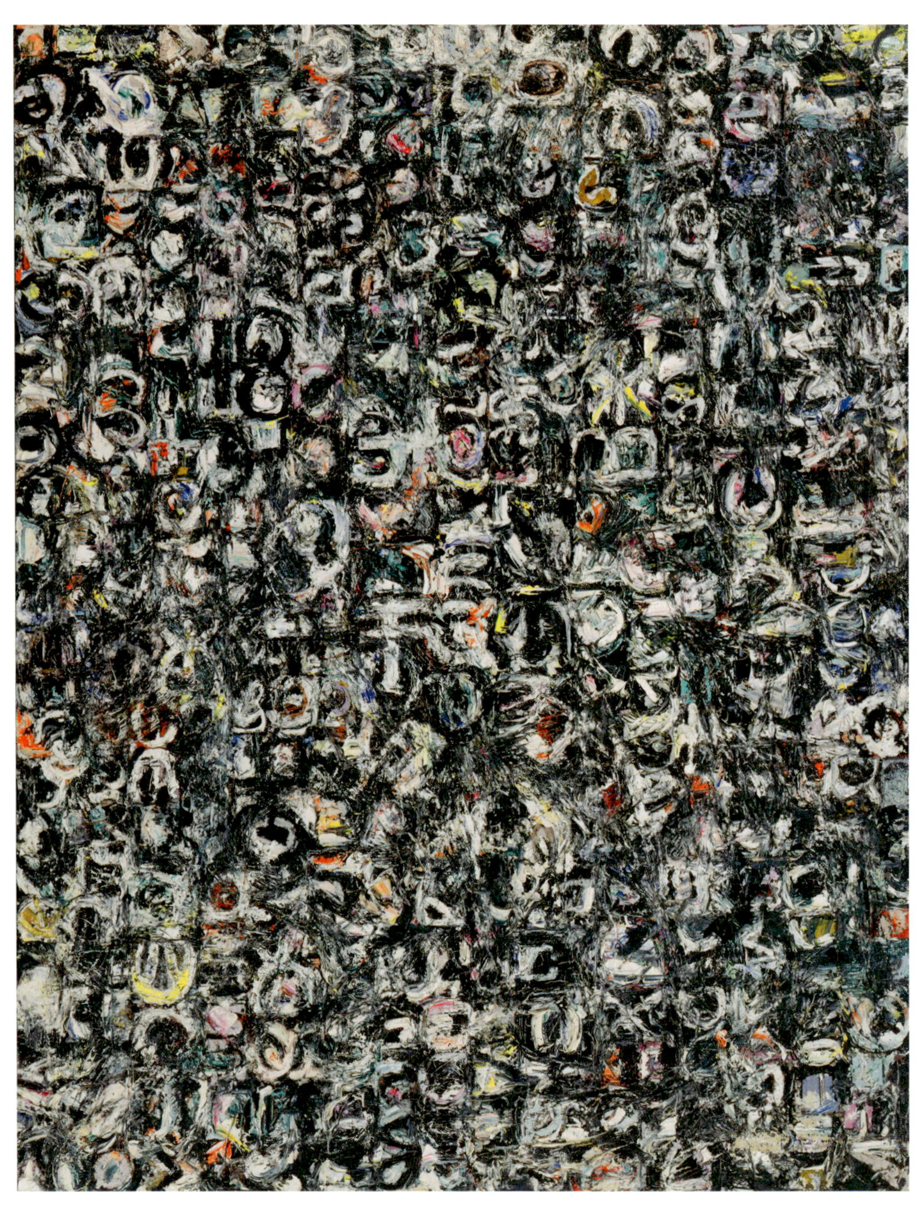

LEE KRASNER, *Untitled*, 1949. Oil on composition board, 48 × 37 in. (121.9 × 94 cm). The Museum of Modern Art, New York, Gift of Alfonso A. Ossorio.

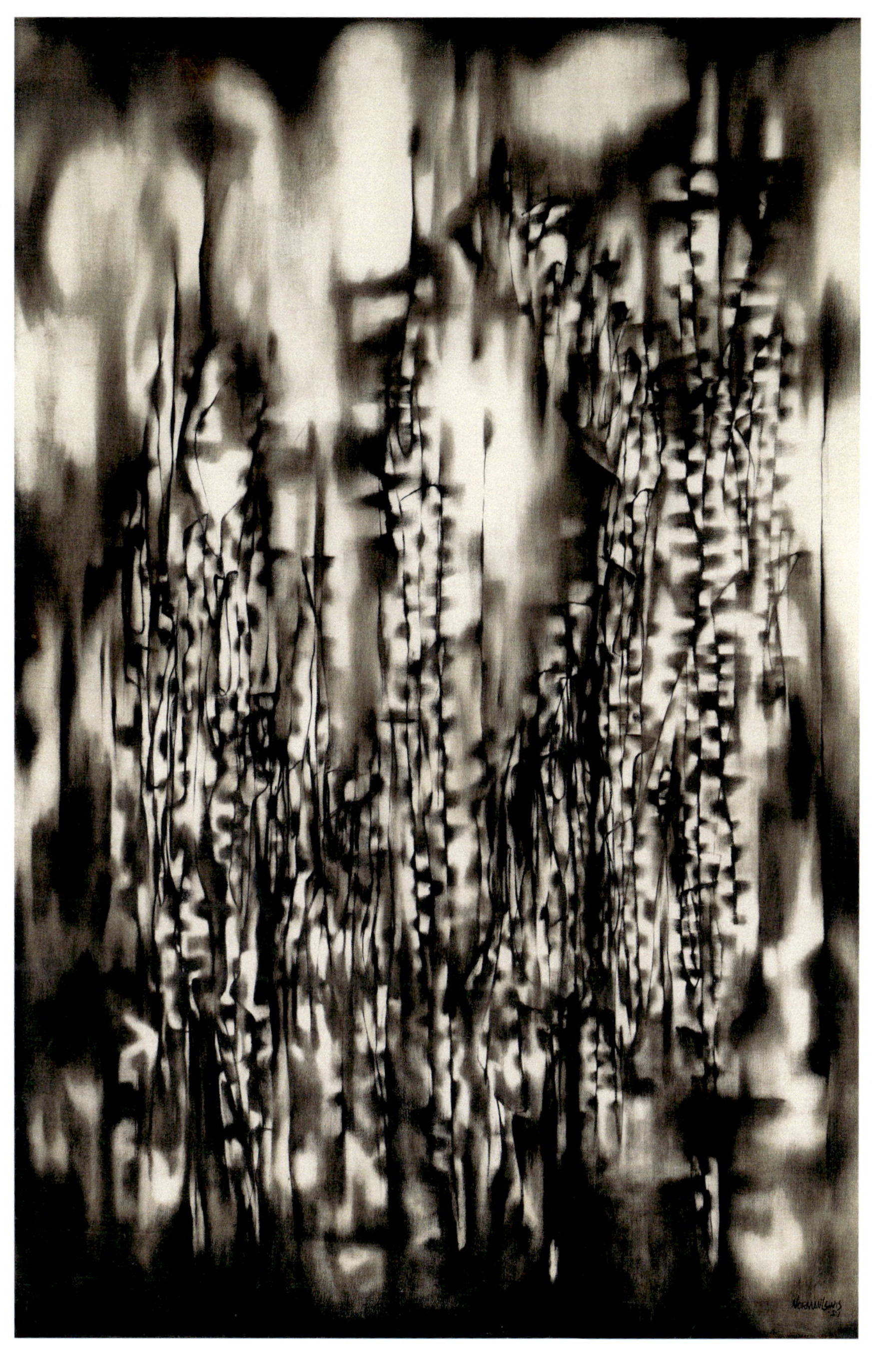

NORMAN LEWIS, *Every Atom Glows: Electrons in Luminous Vibration*, 1951. Oil on canvas, 54 × 35 in. (137.2 × 88.9 cm).
Museum of Fine Arts, Boston, The John Axelrod Collection–Frank B. Benis Fund, Charles H. Bayley Fund, and The Heritage Fund for a Diverse Collection.

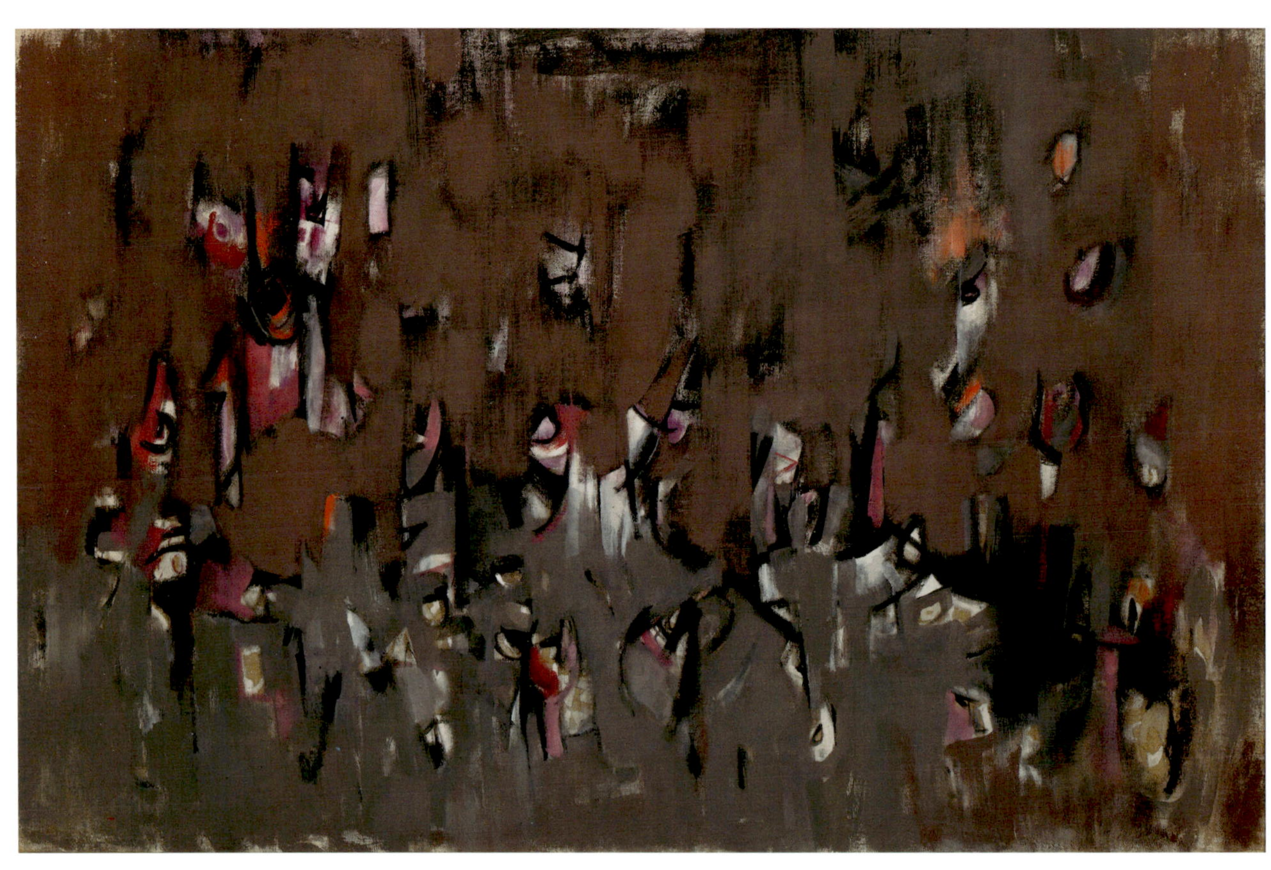

NORMAN LEWIS, *Untitled*, 1958–60. Oil on canvas, 38 × 57 in. (96.5 × 144.8 cm).
Collection of Raymond J. McGuire.

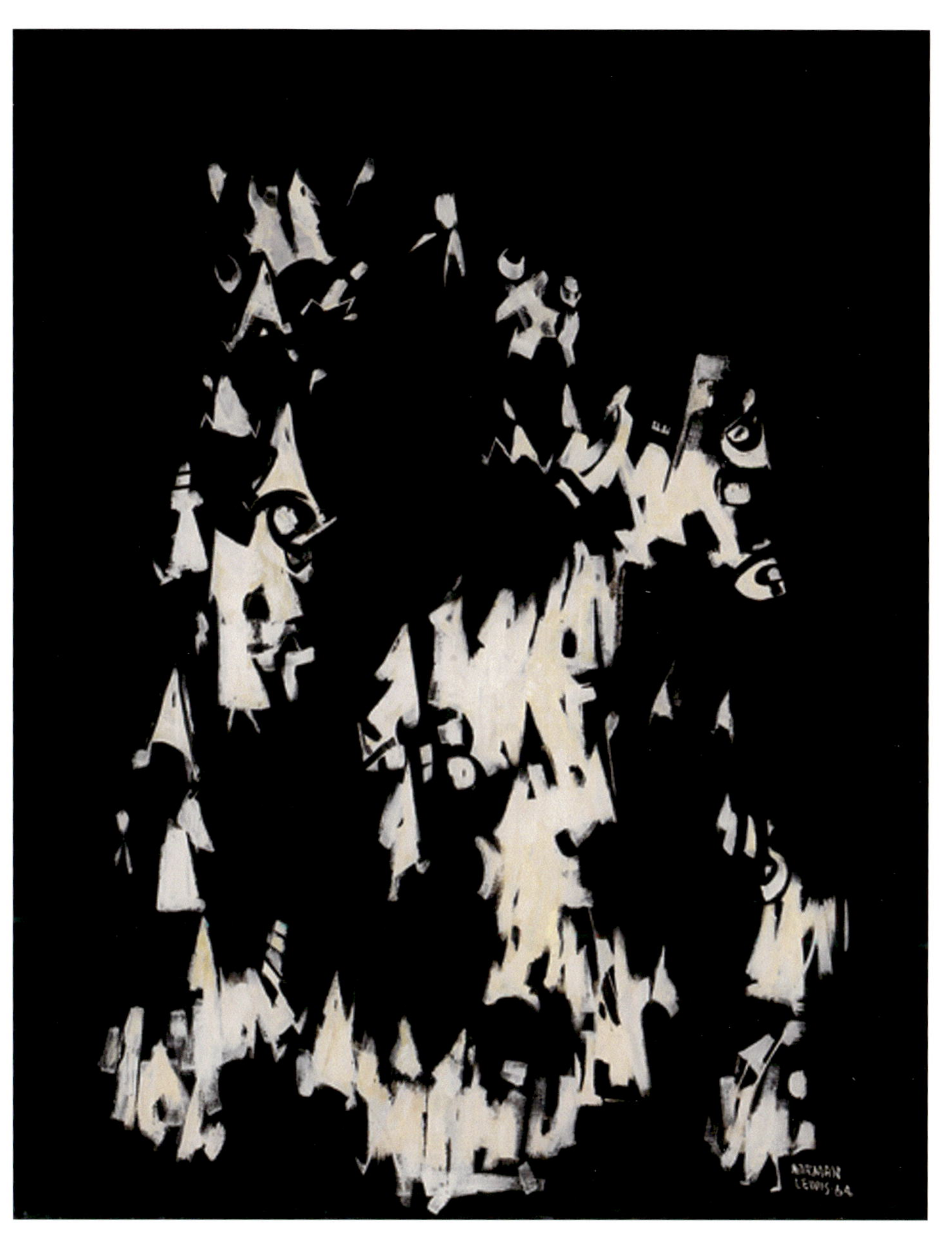

NORMAN LEWIS, *Post Mortem*, 1964. Oil on canvas, 64 × 50 in. (162.6 × 127 cm).
Virginia Museum of Fine Arts, gift of the Fabergé Society.

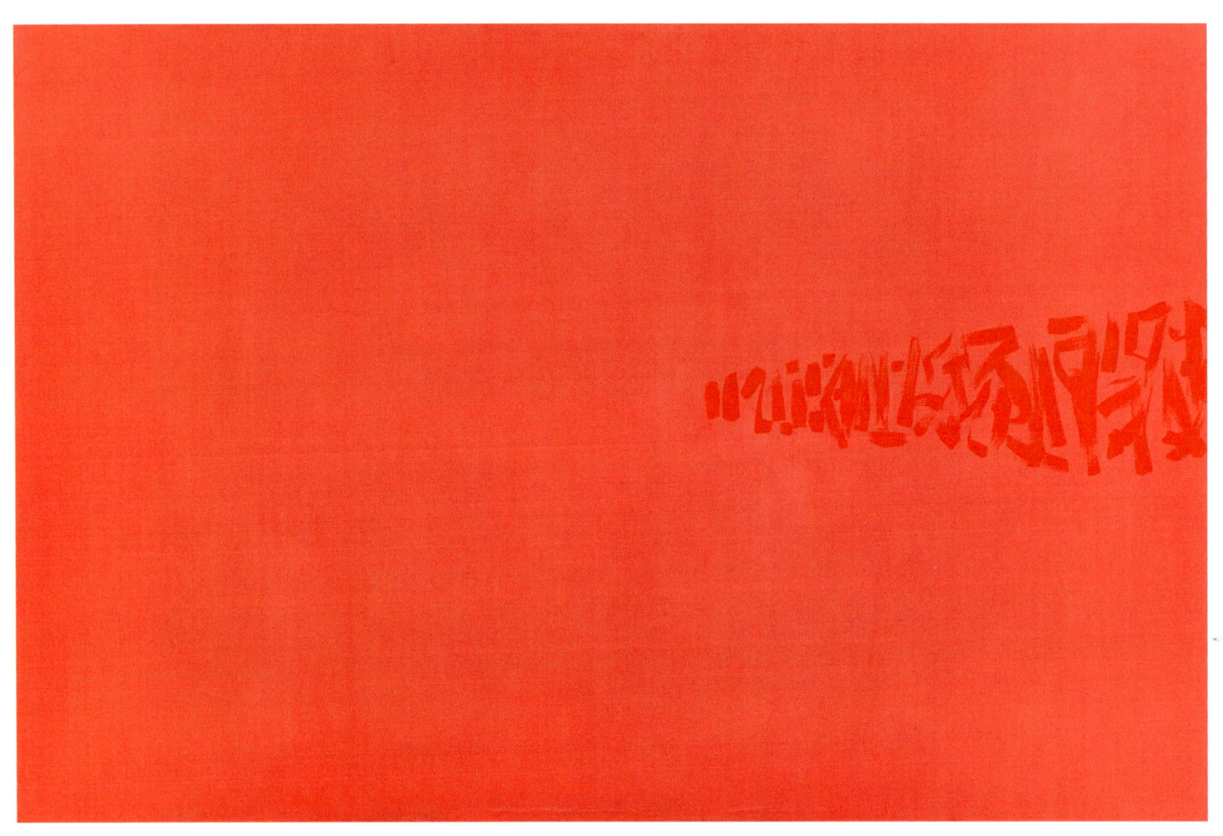

NORMAN LEWIS, *Alabama II*, 1969. Oil on canvas, 48 × 71½ in. (121.9 × 181.6 cm).
Birmingham Museum of Art, Alabama, Promised gift of Bill Hodges Gallery.

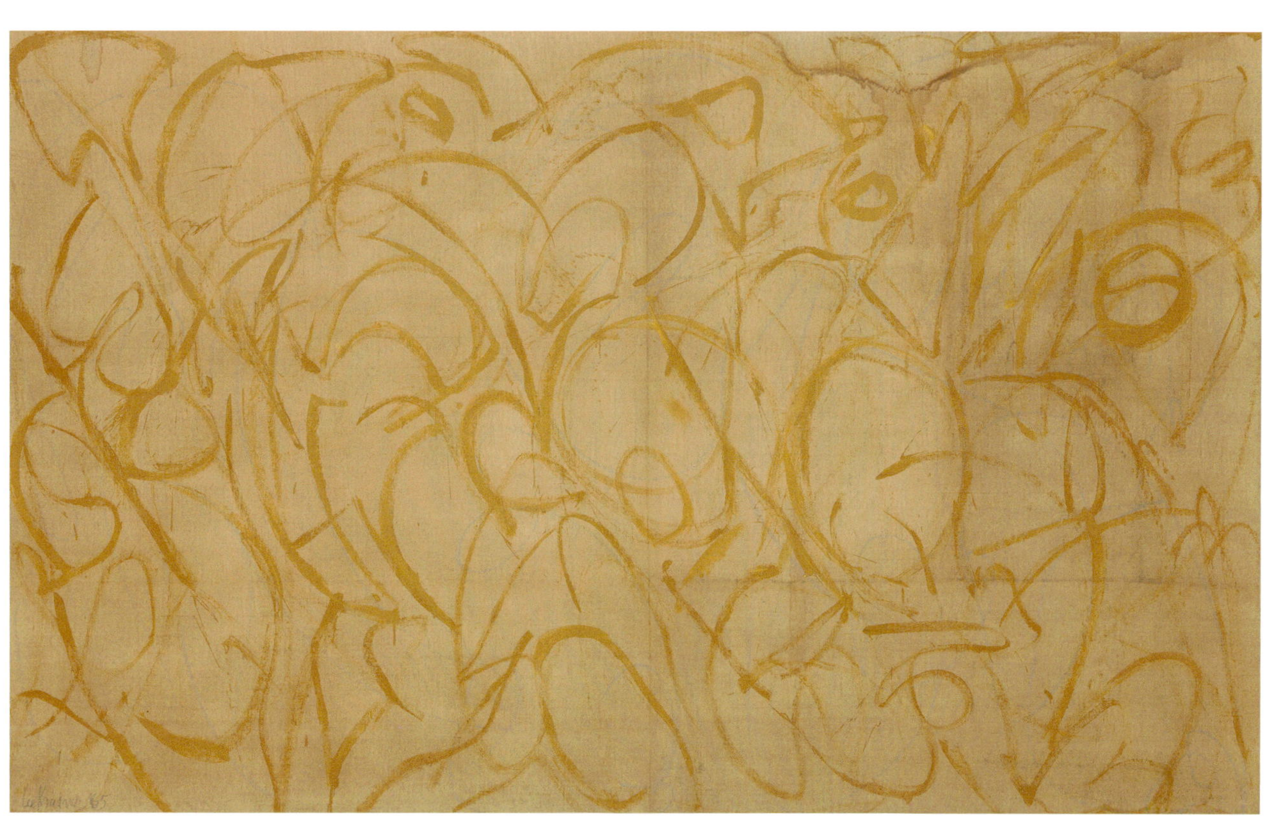

LEE KRASNER, *Kufic*, 1965. Oil on canvas, 81 × 128 in. (205.7 × 325.1 cm).
Courtesy of Robert Miller Gallery, New York.

MYSTERIOUS WRITINGS

LONER IN THE DARK

MYSTERIOUS WRITINGS: ON LEE KRASNER'S LITTLE IMAGES AND THE LANGUAGE OF ABSTRACTION

lisa saltzman

The only thing I can say with absolute assurance is that my "Little Image" work starts about 1946 and ends in 1949.

—lee krasner

This is all, at least at first, that Lee Krasner was willing to concede when, in the context of a conversation with the critic Cindy Nemser, she was pressed to consider the significance of her series of roughly forty small-format, intricately wrought abstractions. Over the course of the interview, however, Krasner relaxed her initial resistance and said a bit more about these diminutive canvases, allover paintings created in a small upstairs bedroom of the house she shared with Jackson Pollock in Springs, Long Island. Her subsequent words largely followed her interlocutor's lead. When Nemser suggested, for example, of one of the more calligraphic of the variously poured, dripped, or painted canvases that "there is a hieroglyphic-like motif which makes one think of ancient symbols of the past," Krasner adopted Nemser's use of the term hieroglyphic in her more expansive response: "Well, I think it does suggest hieroglyphics of some sort. It is a preoccupation of mine from way back and every once in a while it comes into my work again. For instance, in my 1968 show at the Marlborough I have a painting called *Kufic*, [referring to] an ancient form of Arabic writing (see page 65). Every once in a while I fall back to what I call my mysterious writings. I have no idea what this is about but it runs through periods of my work."[1]

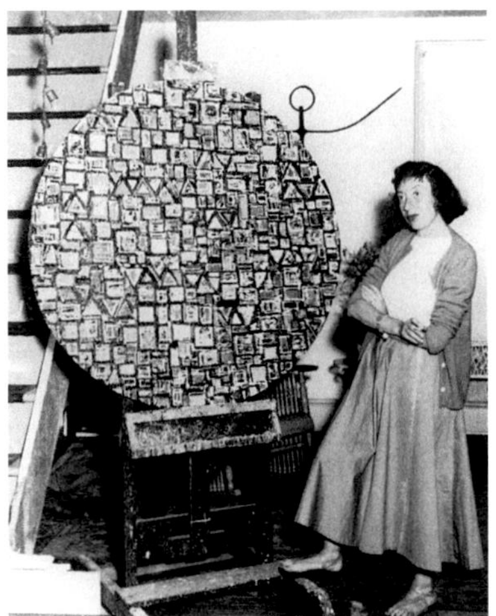

Lee Krasner with *Stop and Go*, c. 1949.

They are not much to go on, these retrospective musings of an aging artist, particularly when they are understood to be prompted by a purposeful critic. And if there is any consensus about the calligraphic impulse in Krasner's paintings, as evinced most expressly and pervasively in the tight rows and dense clusters of linear and geometric characters that cover the surfaces of some number of the Little Image paintings, it seems to stem in large part from another encounter in that same period of the early 1970s, this time with the curator Marcia Tucker in the lead-up to the Whitney Museum's 1973 exhibition of Krasner's so-called Large Paintings, a collection of monumental abstractions created during the prior decade. In the course of their conversation, Tucker observed that it seemed to her as if the paintings had been created from right to left, like Hebrew script. Not only did Krasner readily acknowledge that she had, indeed, albeit not consciously, been working out her Large Paintings in this manner, she also realized that the same held true for an earlier series of abstractions, namely, the small paintings that many consider to be among her finest, the Little Images.[2]

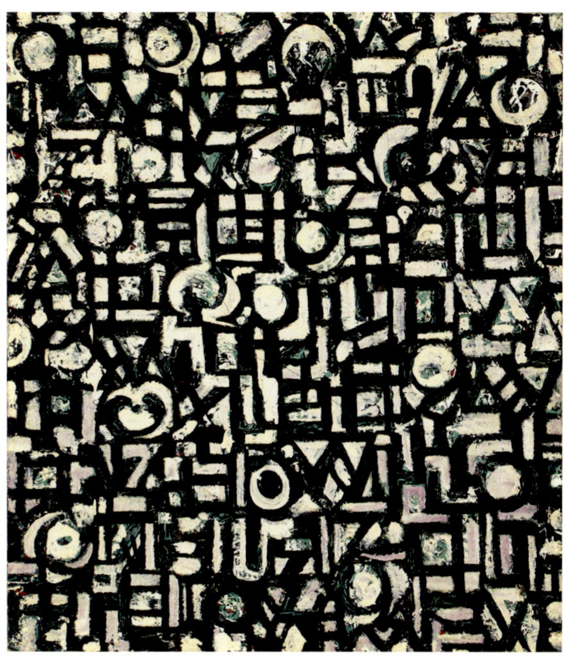

Lee Krasner, *Untitled*, 1949. Oil on canvas, 38 × 33⅛ in. (96.5 × 84.1 cm). Private collection.

Tucker's perspicacious observation, together with knowledge of Krasner's Jewish origins, suddenly supplied a context for the "mysterious writings" that structure and animate the surfaces of her late 1940s abstractions. Lee Krasner may have assimilated the lessons of European modernism, from Henri Matisse to Pablo Picasso to Piet Mondrian, as she studied with, among others, the German émigré painter Hans Hofmann. She may have married in a church and committed to life with the abstract expressionist painter Jackson Pollock, first in an apartment in Manhattan, then in an old farmhouse in East Hampton. In the end, however, it was her childhood exposure to the Hebrew prayer books of her Russian immigrant parents that art historians would latch onto in order to explicate her runic paintings and unlock their secrets.

Yet this reductive turn to biography in the service of iconography, particularly so in the obdurate face of Krasner's mature abstractions, feels incompletely satisfying as a way of thinking about the artist's "mysterious writings," the putative hieroglyphics that line the surfaces of her canvases. Certainly, biography is somehow always there, be it in the immediate reception or the subsequent interpretation of the work, as is true for any woman artist, but particularly for Krasner as the wife of Pollock, that most celebrated of American artists. Indeed, however much scholars may strive to deflate the mythic discourse of masculinity that for so long structured the account of abstract expressionism and, in turn, however that scholarship may seek to read and reclaim the repeated recalibrations of Krasner's oeuvre as masterful moments of painterly control, intellectual rationality, and aesthetic rigor, there lurks the seemingly irreducible fact that she is not just a woman, but a Jewish woman.[3] Despite assimilative strategies or revisionist histories, Lee Krasner will always be, for some, Lena (Lenore) Krassner, Brooklyn born and bred, abstract artist as amanuensis, a latter-day Torah scribe.[4] This is not to say that Krasner's Jewishness does not inflect the creation of her paintings, or, more to the point, that elements of the Hebrew characters that she could recognize but not read do not reappear in the most alphabetic of her Little Images, but I think we might consider the possibility that other influences may inflect their surfaces.

For those scholars who have delved most deeply into Krasner's work, Ellen Landau foremost among them, biography is an absolutely critical part of the interpretive process. That said, even as Landau notes Krasner's formative exposure to Hebrew characters, she ultimately positions that knowledge of a biblical alphabet, and Krasner's attendant familiarity with sacred texts and scrolls, not as a solution to but as a springboard for Krasner's abiding fascination with all sorts of scriptural traditions. There is nothing, for example, in Landau's individual entries in the Krasner catalogue raisonné, the official compendium of the artist's work, to indicate that she regards even a single line or form as a transcription or transfiguration of a Hebrew letter.[5] Instead, Adolph Gottlieb's pictographs and cryptic signs, as well as Mark Tobey's "white writing," general invocations of ancient hieroglyphics, are points of reference as Landau describes and discusses the Little Images—such as *Painting No. 19*, 1947–48; *White Squares*, 1948; and *Composition*, 1949—whose gridded surfaces teem with tight rows of variously linear, angular, or circular geometric forms. Indeed, for Landau, it is ultimately the automatic writing of the surrealists, as enacted in the games of Exquisite Corpse that Krasner played with Pollock, William and Ethel Baziotes, and Maria and Robert Motherwell in the early 1940s, as well as an influential essay by Kurt Seligmann, "Magic Circles," published in *View* magazine in 1942, featuring a chart of Cornelius Agrippa's occult signs, that begins at least to describe the context from

and typography, with letters set in striking arrangements across the dynamic geometries of their overlapping pictorial planes.[7] There is perhaps no more striking example than the 1942 composition *Cryptography*, with its jumble of letters repeated and resolved in the bold banner of text that projects in an almost cinematic beam across the picture's surface, perhaps announcing a solution to the enigma that was then being worked out by the young men and women who stand earnestly before the gridded blackboards, striving to outwit the enemy by creating and deciphering code.

Third, these wartime projects were not the only contemporary arena of cryptanalysis. Over the course of the 1940s, a sequence of important breakthroughs occurred in the quest to decode the

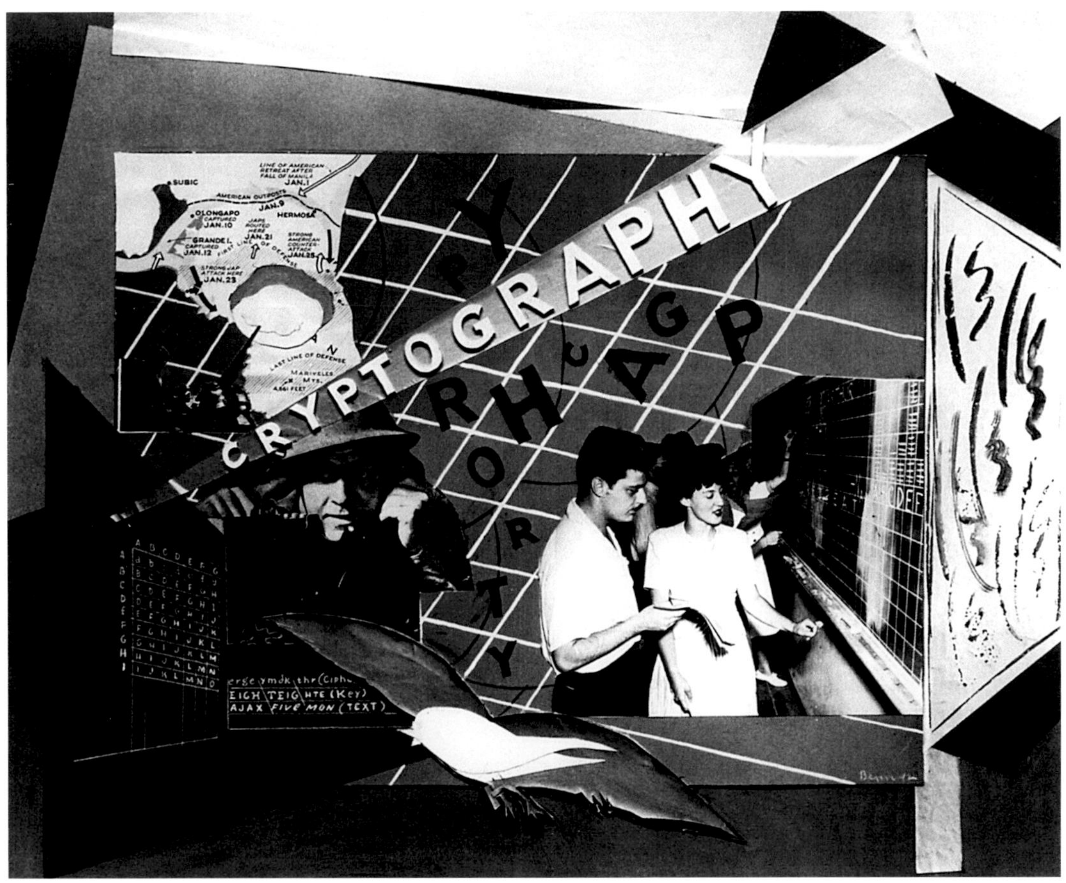

Lee Krasner, *Cryptography*, from the War Services Windows, 1942, destroyed.
Photomontage and collage, dimensions unknown.

enigmatic inscriptions on a set of tablets that had been unearthed in, of all places, Knossos, the heart of ancient Minoan culture that so fueled the imagination of the surrealists and those artists, like Pollock and Krasner, who followed in their wake. Of course, none of the explorers of the unconscious, from the founding figures of psychoanalysis to the artists most inspired by their theories, would have developed their methods or their metaphors without the work of modern archaeologists, from Germany's Heinrich Schliemann at Mycenae to Britain's Arthur Evans on Crete. The discoveries of Evans have a particular relevance here, for his archaeological dig at Knossos at the beginning of the previous century revealed more than just the ruins of the palace of Minos and the Bronze Age civilization that flourished there more than one thousand years before the so-called Classical Age of Greek culture. Evans's work also unearthed a remarkable trove of clay tablets, hardened and preserved by the fire that destroyed the palace of the maritime empire in about 1400 B.C.; these tablets were covered in the linear strokes of an unknown script that he would name Linear B. The mysterious writing inscribed in orderly rows across the lined surfaces of the charcoal-gray tablets would challenge archaeologists and amateurs, classicists and cryptanalysts for more than five decades, but never more so than in the final decade leading up to its triumphant translation in 1952.[8]

Despite working with the tablets until his death in 1941, Evans himself never managed to decipher the script. As any linguist, archaeologist, or cryptanalyst will attest, it is a daunting task to unravel an unknown language written in an unknown script. No one knew that better than a classicist by the name of Alice Kober, a professor of Greek and Latin who dedicated her scholarly life to the historical puzzle of Linear B. As we now know from the archival work of the linguist and journalist Margalit Fox, when Kober was not busy fulfilling her pedagogical duties at Brooklyn College, she worked relentlessly to decipher Linear B. Sitting at the dining room table of her house in Brooklyn, even, at times, her basement Ping-Pong table, she pored over reproductions of drawings and photographs of the ancient tablets, isolating and inventorying their characters and registering both their frequency and patterns of appearance. Ultimately, in the course of generating and working with hundreds of thousands of file cards, compiling an exhaustive list of symbols and devising a system of grids, she developed a method of analysis that would allow her to determine several fundamental properties of the mysterious script, foremost among them, that Linear B was inflected. But it was not until the mid- to late 1940s, after a fellowship from the Guggenheim Foundation allowed her to take time off from her teaching duties and travel to Oxford to see Evans's photographs and drawings of more than two hundred unpublished tablets, that Kober made and published the deductive discoveries that would allow for the decipherment of the enigmatic logograms of the ancient syllabic script.

Sadly, Kober became gravely ill and died in the spring of 1950, at the age of forty-three. The ultimate glory of solving the linguistic puzzle went not to her but to an English architect and amateur cryptanalyst by the name of Michael Ventris, who, in part building on Kober's hard work and important insights, finally cracked the code in 1952.

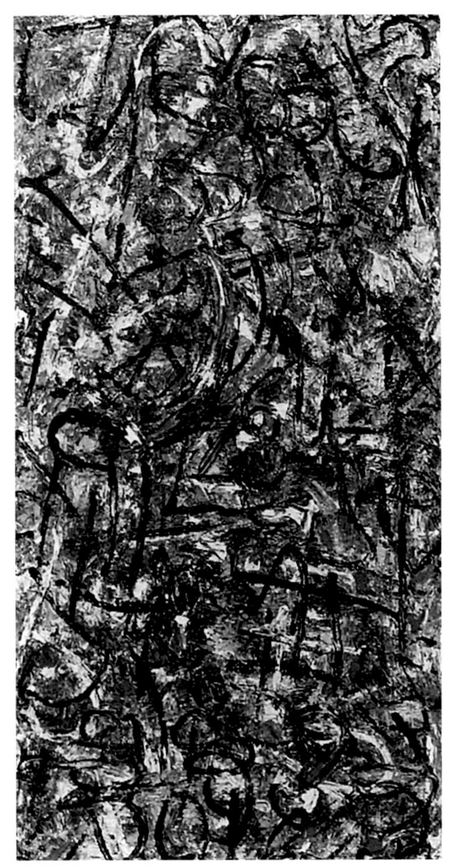

Lee Krasner, *Untitled*, 1946–47. Oil on canvas, 42 × 21¼ in. (106.7 × 54 cm). Location unknown.

To be clear: there is nothing in the historical record to link Alice Kober to Lee Krasner. If anything, it was the solitary scholar, living with her mother in a house in Brooklyn, traveling only in the interest of her research, who might have heard of Krasner, even if only as the wife of that most famous of postwar American artists, Jackson Pollock. That said, the parallels between the two women are remarkable, even uncanny. Both were born to immigrant parents in New York in the first decade of the twentieth century, Krasner to Russian parents in 1908, Kober to Hungarian parents in 1906. Both sought to be educated in ways that were utterly untraditional for their time: Krasner at Cooper Union, the Art Students League of New York, and the National Academy of Design; Kober at Hunter College and Columbia University. Both did extraordinary, truly groundbreaking work in their fields only to be eclipsed by male peers, Krasner by Pollock, Kober by Ventris. Further, although Kober predeceased Ventris (indeed, her illness and untimely death may be the only reason she did not finally crack the code), and Krasner lived and worked for several decades after Pollock's death, even coming to earn something of her due (largely thanks to the women's movement and feminist scholarship in the 1970s), it remains that, for all their contributions to their respective fields, modern art and classics, the real glory went to two men who each died not long after his most resounding period of public acclaim.[9] Of course, Kober's Knossos is not Krasner's. Mythic tales of the Minoan culture of Crete may fuel the imaginations of artists, but that does not automatically make a historical civilization and its script, Linear B, the "source" for Krasner's mysterious writings. Then again, who can say it isn't? What if, on an evening in June of 1946, Lee Krasner happened to attend a lecture at Hunter College in Manhattan? What if she sat in an auditorium and heard a scholar by the name of Alice Kober speak the following words?

> On every kind of writing material known to man, on paper, parchment, papyrus, palm-leaves, on wood, on clay, brick or stone, on every kind of metal, there exist inscriptions which cannot be read. . . . These documents range in date all the way from Neolithic times to the present. Some are probably in the process of being written at this very moment.[10]

At that same moment, Krasner was on the brink of embarking on the painterly project that would become her Little Images. Among the first of these was *Untitled*, c. 1946–47, a painting that is neither signed nor dated and is no longer extant, probably destroyed. A heavily impastoed vertical canvas, the composition is covered in calligraphic signs and symbols. Krasner would soon tighten these stenographic figures into the geometric script, the "hieroglyphs" that came to typify so many of the small, abstract canvases of the following few years. Evocative of, but ultimately utterly distinct from, the ancient language that is Linear B, or, for that matter, biblical Hebrew, the characters that surface on Krasner's abstractions signal a pictorial language all their own, even if they remain, like so many enigmatic artifacts before them, "inscriptions that cannot be read." Abstract art, as we know from Stephen Bann, among others, is not, in its relation to meaning, a language.[11] Yet Krasner's Little Images make us want to believe that it might be, if only we could crack the code.

NOTES

The epigraph is from Cindy Nemser, *Conversations with 12 Women Artists* (New York: Charles Scribner's Sons, 1975), 89. Of course, for all Krasner's assurance, even the assertion of the years 1946–49 is not quite right, as *Untitled (Little Image)*, considered the last of the Little Images, dates to 1950.

1. Nemser, *Conversations*, 90.

2. Marcia Tucker, *Lee Krasner: Large Paintings* (New York: Whitney Museum of American Art, 1973).

3. Anne Wagner, "Lee Krasner as L. K.," *Representations* 24 (Winter 1989): 42–57; Anna Chave, "Pollock and Krasner: Script and Postscript," *Res* 24 (Autumn 1993): 95–111; and Griselda Pollock, "Cockfights and Other Parades: Gesture, Difference, and the Staging of Meaning in Three Paintings by Zoffany, Pollock, and Krasner," *Oxford Art Journal* 26, no. 2 (2003): 143–54.

4. Gail Levin, "Beyond the Pale: Lee Krasner and Jewish Culture," *Woman's Art Journal* 28, no. 2 (Fall–Winter 2007): 28–34.

5. Ellen G. Landau, *Lee Krasner: A Catalogue Raisonné* (New York: Abrams, 1995).

6. Ellen G. Landau, "Lee Krasner's Early Career, Part Two: The '1940s,'" *Arts Magazine* 56, no. 3 (November 1981): 85.

7. Ellen G. Landau, "Lee Krasner's Early Career, Part One: 'Pushing in Different Directions,'" *Arts Magazine* 56, no. 2 (October 1981): 118–19.

8. Here I am utterly indebted to Margalit Fox's *The Riddle of the Labyrinth: The Quest to Crack an Ancient Code* (New York: Ecco/HarperCollins, 2013). See also Mary Beard's review of Fox's book, "What Was Greek to Them?" *New York Review of Books* 60, no. 19 (December 5, 2013), 25–27.

9. Both Pollock and Ventris died in car accidents, within weeks of one another, in 1956.

10. As cited in Margalit Fox, *Riddle of the Labyrinth*, 86.

11. Stephen Bann, "Abstract Art—A Language?" in *Towards a New Art: Essays on the Background to Abstract Art, 1910–20* (London: Tate Gallery, 1980), 125–45. Bann turns to the work of Ernst Gombrich and Claude Levi-Strauss to pursue not what abstraction means, but how it means. As such, Bann's concern is ultimately not to demonstrate that abstract work has meaning and more to suggest that in its morphology, it simulates the structure of meaningful discourse.

LONER IN THE DARK: THE SINGULAR VISION OF NORMAN LEWIS AND THE EVIDENCE OF THINGS UNSEEN

mia l. bagneris

I'm a loner and paint out of a certain self-imposed remoteness.
—**norman lewis**

In 1976, Anthony Barboza, a young but already established African American photographer, captured a haunting likeness of painter Norman Lewis. In this evocative image, Lewis poses alone in front of a flat backdrop, a solitary figure before Barboza's lens. Although most of his face is shrouded in shadow, Lewis's eyes, weary yet determined, catch the light, allowing the artist's visage to emerge from compositional obscurity. His gaze—simultaneously challenging and curious—connects with the viewer, establishing an intimacy and demanding a certain recognition, as if to say, "Can you see me?"

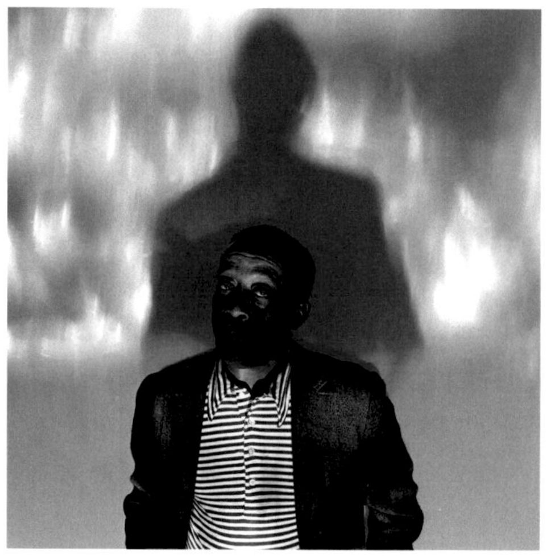

Anthony Barboza, *Norman Lewis—Painter*, 1976. Gelatin silver print.

In the background, amid the dreamscape of an ethereal milieu that recalls the composition of many of Lewis's abstract works, a wraithlike silhouette—Lewis's own ghostly shadow—presides over the photograph from on high. Barboza reverses formal convention, posing his central subject primarily in darkness, bathing the background in heavenly light. Enveloped in this incandescent aura, both artist and apparition comprise a dark center from which exudes an eerily luminescent glow. Made just three years before Lewis's death, Barboza's spectral double portrait can be understood as an

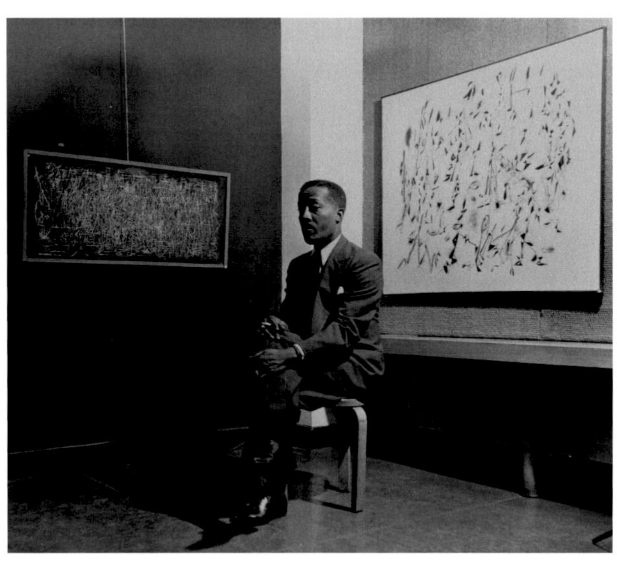

Norman Lewis c. 1950.

illuminating metaphor for the artist's life, offering the viewer a vision of the artist as an enigmatic presence at the center of it all. In order to see him fully, we might have to adjust our vision and reorient our expectations.

A 1997 *New York Times* review of a posthumous gallery show of Lewis's work characterized the painter as "one of those artists best known for not being as well known as he should be."[1] Despite being an undeniable presence—and arguably an important one—at the center of both the burgeoning African American and abstract expressionist art scenes of the early to mid-twentieth century, Lewis remains a shadowy figure relative to both. Ultimately as much apart from both circles as he was a part of them, he was his own center. This vision of himself as an independent loner may have made it difficult for Lewis's contemporaries to "see" him or his achievements as their own.

PAINTING BLACK (OR MAYBE NOT) IN NEW YORK'S BLACK "METROPOLIS": NORMAN LEWIS IN HARLEM The son of Bermudian immigrants, Lewis grew up on Lenox Avenue near 132nd Street and spent the vast majority of his life in Harlem, maintaining a home and studio there for most of his career.[2] He had harbored artistic aspirations since childhood and had studied drawing and commercial design in high school. Lewis received little encouragement from his parents, however, and it was not until he was in his early twenties, when he discovered the thriving black arts community associated with the Harlem Renaissance, that he seriously considered a career as a professional artist.[3] Around 1933, he met the influential black sculptor and art teacher Augusta Savage, whose Savage Studio of Arts and Crafts, located in a basement on West 143rd Street, became a mecca for young black artists. Lewis spent hours honing his skills at Savage's studio, although less, he would later insist, through formal instruction than by observation and trial and error. It was through Savage that the budding painter found a supportive artistic community, becoming deeply enmeshed in Harlem's artistic circles and developing relationships with other African American artists that he would maintain for more than forty years. A fixture in the African American art community, Lewis regularly attended the informal salon known as 306, which met at Charles Alston's 141st Street studio of the same address,[4] was a founding member of the Harlem Artists Guild, and taught at the Harlem Community Arts Center.[5]

Although Lewis, who took classes at Columbia University during the mid-1930s, did pursue other formal avenues of study after working with Savage, the artist preferred the guarantee of independence afforded him by a self-directed course of study.[6] Still, the primarily self-taught painter made extraordinary progress during the early to mid-1930s and in 1936 was accepted into the Federal Art Project of the Works Progress Administration, first as a student and then as a paid art instructor. During this time, Lewis, like many artists in the WPA, worked in a social realist mode, dedicating his art to exposing the plight of poor and working-class men and women while also asserting their humanity and affirming the dignity of labor; as a black artist, still influenced by Harlem Renaissance–era concerns with expressing racial character and solidarity through discernibly "Negro" art, he concentrated his efforts on the depiction of black life.[7] Painting pictures with titles such as *Washerwoman*, *Johnny the Wanderer*, and *Dispossessed*, Lewis dutifully rendered struggling black domestics, destitute drifters, and otherwise dispossessed African Americans. However, with its cubist sensibilities, experimental patches of non-naturalistic color, and figures simplified to the point of near abstraction, even Lewis's social realist work betrays the artist's interest in painters of the European avant-garde and foreshadows his later privileging of formal concerns over political ideology. Not even the dreariness of his social realist subject matter can eclipse the energy of his formal exploration in these scenes. He might, for example, introduce a marvelous compositional tension in the play of angle against curve by contrasting the round swell of a generous bosom with the sharp corners of a washboard, or achieve a similar dynamism by using hanging laundry and the oblique grid of a brick floor to create an energetic ping-pong of intersecting orthogonals.

Throughout the late 1930s and early 1940s, formal interests increasingly found their way into Lewis's painting.[8] By the mid-1940s, he was thoroughly disenchanted with social realism, bristling against what he described as "the limitations which every American Negro who is desirous of a broad kind of development must face, namely the limitations which come under the names 'African Idiom,' 'Negro Idiom,' or 'Social Painting.'"[9] He further observed, "I used to paint Negroes being dispossessed, discrimination, and slowly I became aware of the fact that this didn't move anybody, it didn't make things better."[10]

This shift signaled more than Lewis's frustration at the failure of artistic efforts to effect real change. His reference to the "limitations" with which he contended reveals the extent to which the artist felt deeply constrained and resentful of the expectations placed upon him as a black artist, and Ann Eden Gibson asserts that "Lewis's new [more abstract] painting responded resistantly to the differences he must have long recognized between the imperatives for Black and White artists."[11] Like his white peers of the New York School, many of whom he had met while working in the WPA or through his association with the Artists Union of New York, Lewis recognized the canvas as the space of its own reality brought into being by the act of painting: "Painting, like music, had something inherent in itself which I had to discover and which has nothing to do with what exists, it has another kind of reality, that which is inherent in painting, in those four sides."[12] A few of these early ventures in abstraction—works such as *Composition 1* of 1945, a meticulous étude of color and geometry—investigate the potential of purely nonrepresentational art. Still, comparing works with similar themes such as *Street Musicians* or *Untitled (Jazz Club)*, both from 1945, to 1947's *Twilight Sounds* (see page 33) or 1950's *Street Music* indicates that the artist often continued to maintain some degree of discernible figuration even as he turned toward increasing levels of abstraction over time. These paintings also demonstrate Lewis's transition to allover compositions distinguished by delicate, almost calligraphic painterly gestures, a unique style that would define his oeuvre for the rest of his career.

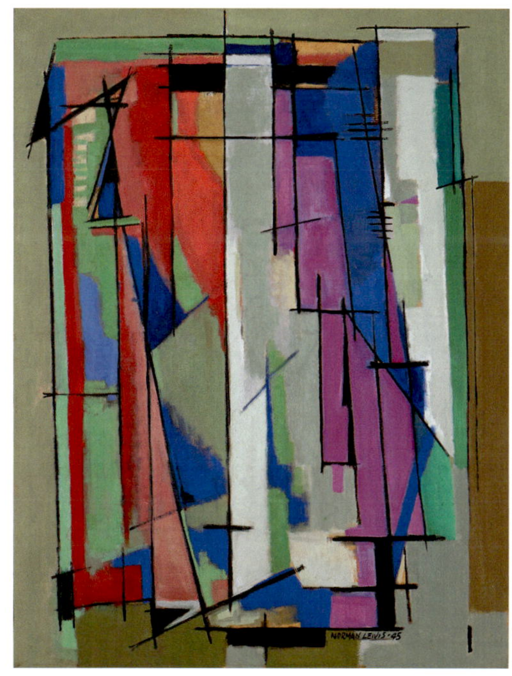

Norman Lewis, *Composition 1*, 1945. Oil on canvas, 35 × 25 in. (88.9 × 63.5 cm). Indianapolis Museum of Art, The Thomas Collection.

Although Lewis no longer accepted social realism, blackness did not disappear from his canvases. As the aforementioned musically inspired titles suggest, Lewis's early abstract works often related to the sights and sounds of black culture, namely jazz.[13] This direct experience also manifested in numerous references to both Harlem and nighttime in Lewis's early abstract paintings. Whereas paintings with titles such as *Metropolitan Crowd*, 1946 (see page 55), *Tenement*, 1948, and *Metropolis*, 1952, demonstrate Lewis's interest in tracing the urban environment generally, others, like *Harlem Courtyard*, 1954, and *Harlem Turns White*, 1955, pay homage to the neighborhood and community with which he strongly identified. Joan Murray Weissman, who made her home with the painter from 1945 to 1952, remembered Lewis's particular fondness for Harlem at night:

> He just liked night, especially nighttime with lights. I think it had more to do with growing up in Harlem than anything more. . . . But he really loved the night; he loved going out at night, and he loved walking at night, and he loved the sky with stars in it, and he loved night. He was a night kind of guy.[14]

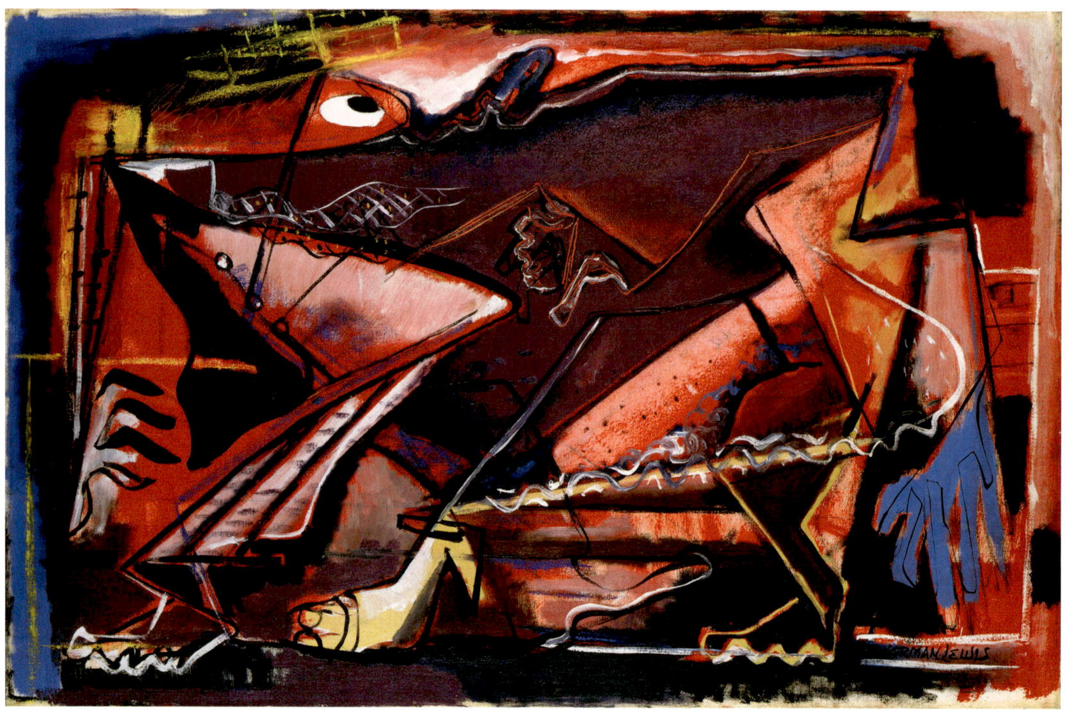

Norman Lewis, *Untitled (Jazz Club)*, 1945. Oil and sand on canvas, 22⅞ × 34½ in. (58.1 × 87.6 cm). Courtesy of Michael Rosenfeld Gallery, New York.

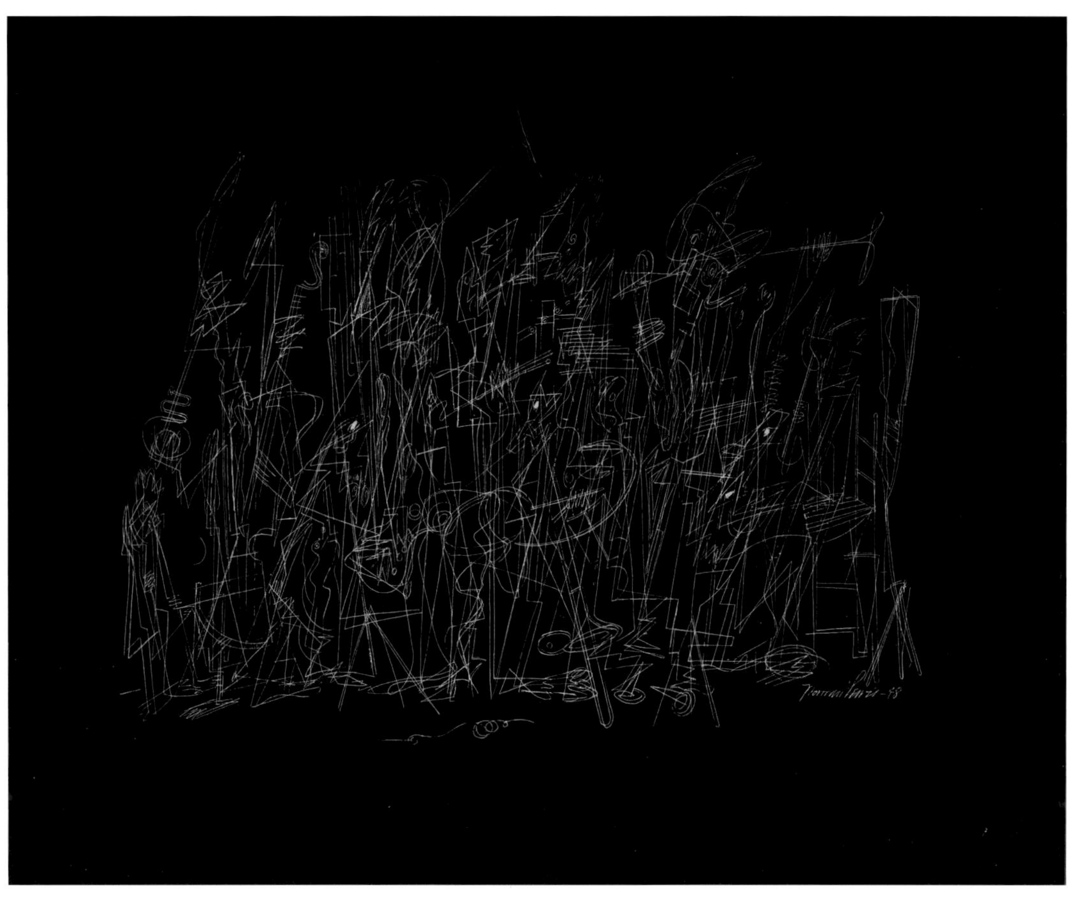

Norman Lewis, *Jazz Band*, 1948. Incised on black-coated masonite, 20 × 23⅞ in. (50.8 × 60.6 cm).
Collection of Rodney M. Miller.

The artist's nocturnal habits also influenced his notoriously somber palette. From his first forays into abstraction until the end of his career, Lewis continually returned to an almost obsessive formal and philosophical consideration of the possibilities of black, resulting in his most well-known body of work, the Black Paintings.[15] Asserting that his chosen color "could have been blue . . . it could have been red," Lewis insisted that his decision to work in black was motivated by purely formal, not racial, concerns.[16] He wanted to observe, for example, how "the brushstroke 'varied in its physical touch on the canvas from light to dark.'"[17] Lewis further explained, "I wanted to see if I could get out of black the suggestion of other nuances of color, using it in such a way as to arouse other colors. . . . This was . . . using color in such a way that it could become other things."[18]

Although several of his Harlem contemporaries pursued abstraction at this time, only Lewis devoted his entire mature career to abstract painting.[19] His decision to leave the "real world" at the studio door and to commit his art solely to the reality of the canvas indicates the extent to which he followed his own course. Bearden and Henderson observed that Lewis "felt extremely isolated in asserting his right to paint as he felt," yet the painter also seems to have accepted his maverick nature with a degree of pride:

> I'm a loner and paint out of a certain self-imposed remoteness. When I'm at work, I usually remove my state of mind from the Negro environment I live in. . . . I paint what's inside, and like to think of it as a very personal, very individual environment. Being Negro, of course, is part of what I feel, but in expressing all of what I am artistically, I often find myself in a visionary world, to which 125th Street would prove limited and less than universal by comparison.[20]

ALONE IN A CROWD: NORMAN LEWIS AND THE NEW YORK SCHOOL Even in a crowd, Lewis was often arguably alone, as evidenced by an oft-repeated anecdote: in 1950, he was the only African American painter invited to take part in the legendary Artists' Sessions at Studio 35, a series of roundtable discussions in which thirty-five artists (including, among others, Willem de Kooning, Robert Motherwell, Barnett Newman, and Lewis's close friend Ad Reinhardt) hashed out the meaning of mid-century American avant-garde painting. Recognizing the subtle distinction between art divorced from social statements and the artist as an individual divorced from society, Lewis asked the group to comment upon the relationship and responsibility of the artist to the outside world.[21] Lewis's inquiry—anathema to the other artists' visions of themselves as responsible only to themselves and, perhaps, each other—met with a deafening silence that not even prompting from his good friend Reinhardt could break. The other artists responded as though Lewis, who was clearly sitting at the same table with them, had not even spoken, as though he were not even there. Max Yavno's famous double photograph chronicling the talks reflects the artist's position—during the discussions and historically—vis-à-vis this formidable group. Rather than standing out as the black dot in a sea of white faces, Lewis's black face, placed at the margin of both images, disappears into the background, his features scarcely discernible in the dim exposure.

Ann Eden Gibson argues that, seated with Lewis at the table, "These artists were in a position to 'see' Norman Lewis and his work, but they shut out any communication that might affect their control of the scene."[22] While agreeing with the main thrust of Gibson's observation, I would like to suggest that these artists, as well as the collectors and critics at this germinal juncture in American art history—too blinded by the privileged position of their own whiteness—were actually in no position to see Lewis or appreciate his work. In a section of his larger essay "Greenberg, Rosenberg, and Postwar American Art," aptly subtitled "Blind Spots," Norman Kleeblatt considers how it was that Lewis, who associated with New York School artists and painted abstract canvases almost exclusively from the mid-1940s until his death, managed to go practically unnoticed by those two critical titans of mid-century abstraction and veritable definers (along with Irving Sandler, who also ignored Lewis) of the roster of accepted abstract expressionist artists.[23] Lewis frequented the Cedar Bar, participated in discussions at the Eighth Street Club,[24] merited an invitation to the Artists' Sessions, was represented by the prestigious Willard Gallery, and was included in formative exhibitions like The Museum of Modern Art's 1951 *Abstract Painting and Sculpture in America*. Given these credentials, Gibson observes that the factors contributing to Lewis's relative obscurity at the time must have been significant.[25]

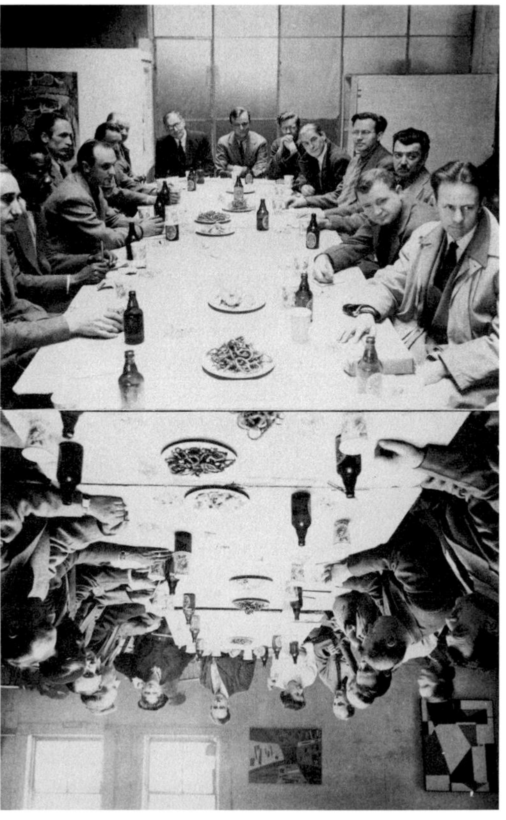

Max Yavno, *Artists' Sessions at Studio 35*, 1950. Gelatin silver print, composite photograph. Art Students League of New York.

Lewis's struggle against a pronounced double blindness—a simultaneous inability of others either to see his blackness or to see past it—contributed to his position as a lonely vanguardist among the avant-garde. Because the avant-garde credo theoretically eschewed any concern with social realities, the fact of Lewis's blackness should have been unimportant; however, such a position failed to recognize the real-world implications of Lewis's race in relationship to an art world in which, especially with the rise of abstract expressionism, collectors fancied themselves as purchasing not just a painting but also a manifestation of the artist's essence. Only later did Lewis and his dealer, Marion Willard, recognize the disadvantage that his socially prescribed absence from certain fashionable scenes, such as parties and dinners with collectors, put the artist. Lewis recalled,

> She very innocently, I think, thought like I did. Art is devoid of prejudice and then some fifteen years later she says to me, "I know I have failed you." What that implied was it was something lacking in promotion or my physical presence to certain environments.[26]

In addition to many failing to see the real impact of Lewis's race, it was also hard for many to see past it. Despite their shared concerns as painters, sometimes even his associates among the New York School had difficulty seeing Lewis as one of their own. Weissman remembers, "They liked Norman; they were glad he was there. . . . But it was a strange attitude: what was he doing there? He should be painting lynchings."[27] Moreover, even when others recognized Lewis's painting as exceptional, they seemed to see it as such either because of or in spite of his race. Pursuing a potential sale, for example, Marion Willard emphasized to the buyer that Lewis had "made a real contribution to painting, perhaps the finest of his race in that it does not deal with social problems but spiritual and painting problems."[28] If, even among this group, Lewis was seen in terms of his Otherness, how could his art ever be seen in terms of the universalism to which abstract expressionism aspired? Yet the most poignant part of Lewis's artistic project was, perhaps, his insistence that his experience, inevitably "Negro" as it was, was as much a part of what constituted "the universal" as the experience of his white peers.[29]

The universality of Lewis's vision may have been overlooked, however, in the delicate linearity of his quiet compositions. As Thomas Lawson observed in the catalogue for the only retrospective Lewis had during his lifetime, the significance of the artist's subtle gestures was hard to see with eyes primed for the larger-than-life ones privileged by critics like Greenberg and Rosenberg: Lewis's "painting appeared vastly economical of means in an era which delighted in fat painting, while the pale, sensitive color and general lyricism of mood that it implied was too easily neglected amidst the large scale dramas of American abstraction."[30] Dwarfed by more luminary giants of mid-twentieth-century painting, Norman Lewis and his lyrical little canvases lingered alone in the shadows.

LONER IN THE DARK: NORMAN LEWIS ON HIS OWN Although he recognized himself as a loner, Lewis often reflected upon the psychology of groups. Particularly interested in the compulsion toward conformity, he observed that "human beings are almost like ants, you know

. . . you notice them going into Macys, everybody goes into the same goddamn doorway waiting for the revolving door yet nobody takes the initiative to open the other door which exists there." Beginning in the late 1940s and continuing at various points throughout his career, Lewis began to paint what he called Little People pictures, exploring the behavior of human nature in groups.[31] In the earliest Little People painting, *Ring Around the Rosie*, 1948, a child's game seems to take a sinister turn as schematic, wraithlike forms rendered in black converge in a circle, closing in around a central figure and an ominous red dot that suggests a spot of blood or, perhaps, the first stone cast. In works with evocative titles such as *Congregation*, 1950, or *Procession in White*, 1953, the calligraphic traces of the artist's brush are rendered as an accumulation of delicate, densely packed strokes, often appearing as figures moving en masse across the canvas. In *Evening Rendezvous*, 1962, peaks of white on a gray-green field stand out like Ku Klux Klan riders rallying around the bonfire of red at the center of the image. Although some works, like *Processional*, 1964, imply a positive vision of group potential, in most, particularly the early examples, Lewis's sympathies align squarely with the loner, his suspicions cast toward the group.

Clearly, Lewis fancied himself the guy who takes the initiative to open "the other door." After opening that door, however, he often found himself alone. Even when he shared the space with other people, he remained outside of their view. Lewis recognized this as a challenging but potentially productive position with which not all artists were prepared to contend:

> And this is where it gets very challenging . . . the question of being alone. . . . I don't think many black cats know how to be alone because it requires this kind of concentration and when you are alone what do you have to say. Do you have anything to say?[32]

With a distinguished career that spanned more than forty years, Norman Lewis clearly had much to say, but it seems unfair to consider the legacy of this self-declared loner only in terms of the groups with which he was affiliated but to which he failed to conform.

While visiting in Crete in 1973, Lewis became fascinated with a mountain visible from the window of his hotel. Sketching it almost obsessively at various times of day, he observed that what really intrigued him was that "the mountain existed at night, too—even though I couldn't see it." Once back at home in his studio, fixated on the reality of the mountain's enduring presence despite his inability to see it, the artist painted a series exploring "the emergence of the mountain in the blackness of night."[33] While he seems to have been cast into the art-historical penumbra of two of the

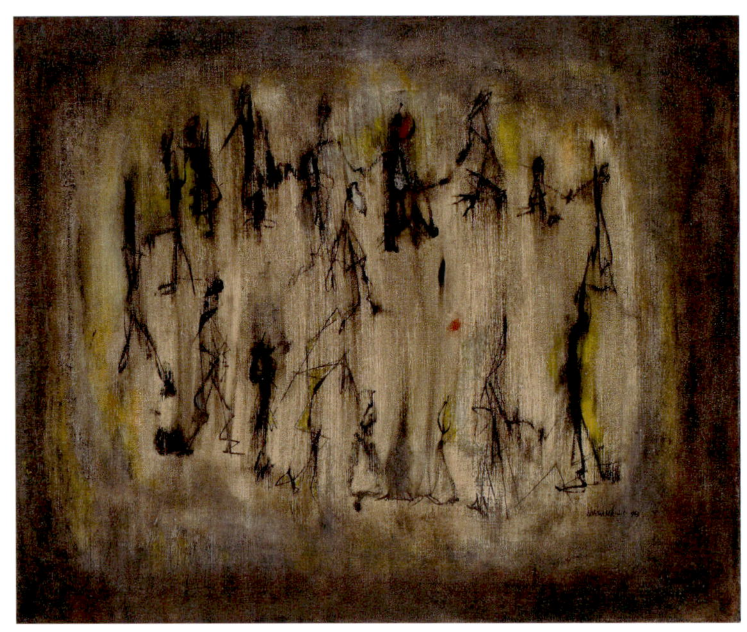

Norman Lewis, *Ring Around the Rosie*, 1948. Oil on canvas, 27 × 32 in. (68.6 × 81.3 cm). Davis Museum and Cultural Center, Wellesley College, Gift of Miriam Mason Wood (Class of 1961) and Charles O. Wood III.

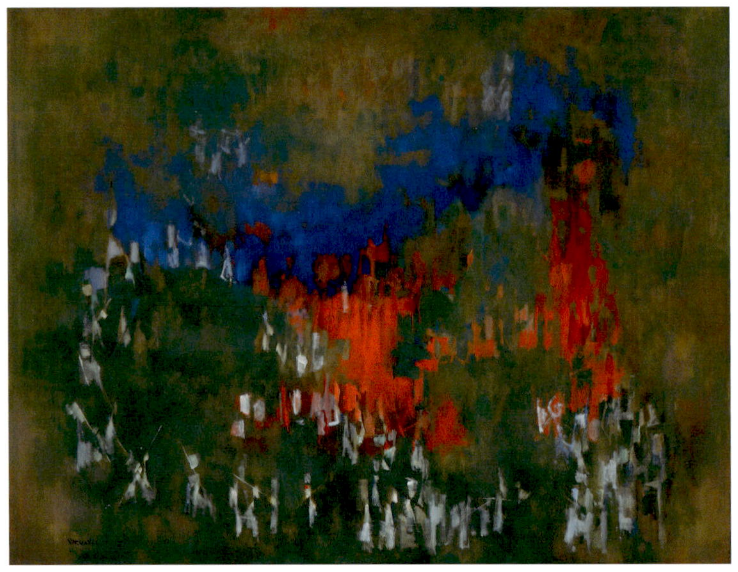

Norman Lewis, *Evening Rendezvous*, 1962. Oil on linen, 50¼ × 64¼ in. (127.7 × 163.3 cm). Smithsonian American Art Museum, Washington, D.C.

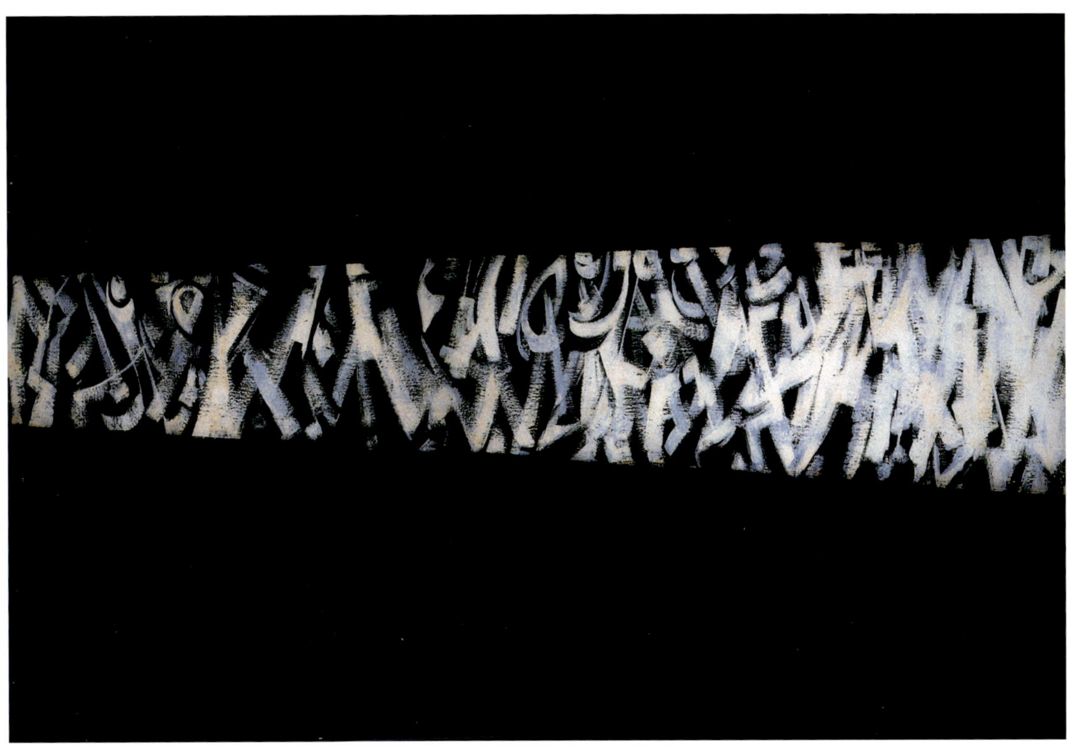

Norman Lewis, *Processional*, 1964. Oil on canvas, 38½ × 57¼ in. (97.8 × 145.4 cm). Private collection.

most luminary developments of twentieth-century American art, the artist's perceptive observations about the mountain offer a useful way to think of his heretofore under-recognized legacy, reminding us that our inability to see something—or, I would like to suggest, someone—of substance cannot diminish its magnitude.

NOTES

The epigraph is quoted in Bearden and Henderson, *A History of African-American Artists* (New York: Pantheon Books, 1993), 324.

1. Barry Schwabsky, "A Forgotten Voice from an Age of Exploration," *New York Times* (February 9, 1997).

2. Most historians date the beginning of the Great Migration, which transformed Harlem into a predominantly black neighborhood, to 1910, the year after Lewis was born. The artist remembered the Harlem of his youth as peopled primarily by Irish, Italian, and Jewish families. See "Oral History Interview with Norman Lewis," July 14, 1968, Archives of American Art, Smithsonian Institution, Washington, D.C.

3. "Oral History Interview with Norman Lewis."

4. Alston shared the studio with the sculptor Henry "Mike" Bannarn and the dancer Ad Bates. Romare Bearden, Jacob Lawrence, and Hale Woodruff were also regular attendees of this informal discussion group, which later evolved into a more formalized venue to support emerging African American artists with black and white supporters. See Sharon F. Patton, *African-American Art* (Oxford and New York: Oxford University Press, 1998), 152.

5. Later, during the 1960s, with Bearden and Ernest Crichlow, Lewis founded the Cinqué Gallery to support the careers of emerging artists of color, and as one of the founding members of Spiral (along with other established Harlem artists such as Alston, Bearden, and Woodruff), he contributed to the group's vibrant debates about the relationship of the black artists to their communities, to the Civil Rights struggle, and to the mainstream art establishment. The Spiral group met from 1963 to 1966, mounting one group show in 1964 that, unbound to a particular political agenda, represented the generational, aesthetic, and conceptual diversity of the group's membership (gender diversity seemed to be less of a concern as the group included only one woman, Emma Amos).

6. Romare Bearden and Harry Henderson implicitly acknowledged the critical importance of artistic independence for Lewis, noting, "His rejection of formal study, Lewis later acknowledged, made his development slower and more difficult than it might have been. *Nevertheless, it guaranteed his independence.*" Bearden and Henderson, *A History of African-American Artists*, 317 (emphasis added).

7. Confirming these sympathies, Lewis's application for a 1942 Rosenwald Fellowship declared his intention "to paint the Negro in Harlem and throughout the South, giving special attention to different forms of labor in different locations. Also depicting the Negro doing his part in the National defense." Quoted in Ann Eden Gibson, "Norman Lewis in the Forties," in *Norman Lewis: From the Harlem Renaissance to Abstraction* (New York: Kenkeleba House, Inc., 1989), 13.

8. See, for example, the sharp planes of color in Lewis's *Washerwoman* and the well-known work *Yellow Hat*, both from 1936, and the fractured planes of nonnaturalistic hues of *Madonna* of 1939.

9. Norman Lewis, "Thesis, 1946," reproduced in *Norman Lewis: From the Harlem Renaissance to Abstraction*, 63.

10. "Oral History Interview with Norman Lewis."

11. Gibson, "Norman Lewis in the Forties," 14.

12. "Oral History Interview with Norman Lewis."

13. Sara Wood has suggested that part of Lewis's marginalization as an abstract expressionist stems from a dismissal of the painter's more direct references to the avant-garde music as too literal, too rooted in a discernible subject, in contrast to the more oblique allusions related to the mystical-metaphoric fascination with bebop expressed by white artists like Jackson Pollock. See Sara Wood, "'Pure Eye Music': Norman Lewis, Abstract Expressionism and Bebop," in Graham Lock and David Murray, eds., *The Hearing Eye: Jazz & Blues Influences in African American Visual Art* (Oxford and New York: Oxford University Press, 2009), 95–119.

14. Joan Murray Weissman, quoted in Ann Eden Gibson, "Black Is a Color: Norman Lewis and Modernism in New York," in *Norman Lewis: Black Paintings, 1946–1977*, exh. cat. (New York: Studio Museum in Harlem, 1998), 18.

15. Kellie Jones organized an exhibition of Lewis's Black Paintings at the Robeson Center Gallery in 1985. In 1989, they were featured in a show at the Studio Museum in Harlem, whose catalogue included essays by Ann Eden Gibson and Jorge Daniel Veneciano, specifically on this aspect of Lewis's oeuvre; see *Norman Lewis: Black Paintings, 1946–1977.*

16. Bearden and Henderson, *A History of African-American Artists*, 321. As

Ann Eden Gibson and others have argued, whether Lewis could admit it or not, he was indeed also interested in black's "effectiveness at referring to a broad range of social and subjective topics," particularly race.

17. Bearden and Henderson, *A History of African-American Artists*, 321.

18. Ann Eden Gibson, "Black Is a Color," 11.

19. During the mid- to late 1940s, Bearden also worked in figurative abstraction. In fact, with representation by the prestigious Kootz Gallery, exhibition at the Whitney Annuals, and works in the permanent collection of The Museum of Modern Art, Bearden could be counted among the more prominent American modernists, white or black, at the time. Hale Woodruff, another of Lewis's contemporaries on the Harlem arts scene, also explored abstraction throughout his career, as did Charles Alston and Beauford Delaney, among others. All of these artists, however, returned to or maintained evidently African American subject matter in their works, and none was committed exclusively to abstract painting.

20. Lewis quoted in Bearden and Henderson, *A History of African-American Artists*, 322, 324.

21. Jorge Daniel Veneciano, "The Quality of Absence in the Black Paintings of Norman Lewis," in *Norman Lewis: Black Paintings, 1946–1977*, 31–41, esp. 36.

22. Ann Eden Gibson, "Recasting the Canon: Norman Lewis and Jackson Pollock," *Art Forum* (March 1992): 72.

23. See Norman L. Kleeblatt, "Blind Spots: Lee Krasner, Grace Hartigan, and Norman Lewis," in Norman L. Kleeblatt, ed., *Action/Abstraction: Pollock, De Kooning, and American Art, 1940–1976*, exh. cat. (New York and New Haven: Jewish Museum and Yale University Press, 2008), 145–50.

24. Also known simply as The Club, the Eighth Street Club refers to the loft at 39 East Eighth Street, where members of the abstract expressionist circle met in the evenings to talk informally as well as listen to speakers and participate in more formal discussions.

25. See Gibson, "Recasting the Canon," 68–69.

26. "Oral History Interview with Norman Lewis."

27. Gibson, "Recasting the Canon," 71.

28. Marion Willard to Robert Beverly Hale, March 15, 1949, quoted in Ann Eden Gibson, *Abstract Expressionism, Other Politics* (New Haven: Yale University Press, 1997), 121.

29. Gibson, "Black Is a Color," 23.

30. Thomas Lawson, *Norman Lewis: A Retrospective* (New York: City University of New York, 1976), unpaginated.

31. "Oral History Interview with Norman Lewis." Lewis also sometimes called them "little figures." See Gibson, "Black Is a Color," 20.

32. "Oral History Interview with Norman Lewis."

33. Bearden and Henderson, *A History of African-American Artists*, 327.

INDEX

Page numbers in italics indicate paintings and photographs.

S

T

U

V

W

Y

ILLUSTRATION CREDITS AND COPYRIGHTS

COPYRIGHTS

Artworks by Lee Krasner © 2014 The Pollock-Krasner Foundation/Artists Rights Society (ARS), New York.

Artworks by Norman Lewis © The Estate of Norman W. Lewis, courtesy of Iandor Fine Arts, New Jersey.

Page 16: Artwork © Romare Bearden Foundation/Licensed by VAGA, NY. Digital image copyright The Museum of Modern Art/Licensed by SCALA/Art Resource, NY. Page 16: Artwork © 2014 Estate of Pablo Picasso/Artists Rights Society (ARS), New York. Page 17: Artwork © 2014 Estate of Ad Reinhardt/Artists Rights Society (ARS), New York. Page 18: Artwork © Successió Miró/Artists Rights Society (ARS), New York/ADAGP, Paris 2014. Page 20: Artwork © 2014 Estate of Mark Tobey/Artists Rights Society (ARS), New York. Page 29: Photograph © Christie's Images Limited 2004. Page 61: Photograph © 2014 Museum of Fine Arts, Boston. Page 69: Photograph © Christie's Images Limited 2013. Page 72: Artwork © 2014 The Pollock-Krasner Foundation/Artists Rights Society (ARS), New York. Page 78: Photograph © Anthony Barboza. Page 85: Photograph © Max Yavno.

EXTENDED CAPTIONS

Page 14: Lee Krasner, *Self-Portrait*, The Jewish Museum, New York. Purchase: Esther Leah Ritz Bequest; B. Gerald Cantor, Lady Kathleen Epstein, and Louis E. and Rosalyn M. Shecter Gifts, by exchange; Fine Arts Acquisitions Committee Fund; and Miriam Handler Fund, 2008-32. Page 16: Romare Bearden: Newark Museum, Gift of Mr. and Mrs. Benjamin E. Tepper, 1946, 46.164. Page 20: Mark Tobey, *New York Tablet*, Munson-Williams-Proctor Arts Institute, Utica, Edward W. Root Bequest. 57.263. Page 21: Lee Krasner, *Imperative*, Gift of Mr. and Mrs. Eugene Victor Thaw, in Honor of the 50th Anniversary of the National Gallery of Art, 1991.59.1. Page 31: Norman Lewis, *Phantasy II*, The Museum of Modern Art, New York, 528.1998. Page 32: Lee Krasner, *Untitled*, Collection of Caryn and Craig Effron, promised gift to The Jewish Museum, New York, P.1.2008. Page 33: Norman Lewis, *Twilight Sounds*, Saint Louis Art Museum, Funds given by Mr. and Mrs. John Peters MacCarthy, Mr. and Mrs. Harvey Saligman, Billy E. Hodges, and the Art Enrichment Fund, 88:2007. Pages 38 and 71: Lee Krasner, *Composition*, Philadelphia Museum of Art: Gift of the Aaron E Norman Fund, Inc., 1959. Page 61: Norman Lewis, *Every Atom Glows: Electrons in Luminous Vibration*, Museum of Fine Arts, Boston. The John Axelrod Collection—Frank B. Bemis Fund, Charles H. Bayley Fund, and The Heritage Fund for a Diverse Collection, 2011.1799. Page 63: Norman Lewis, *Post Mortem*, Virginia Museum of Fine Arts, gift of the Fabergé Society of the Virginia Museum of Fine Arts, 2001.9. Page 73: Lee Krasner, *Cryptography*, Jackson Pollock and Lee Krasner papers, Archives of American Art, Smithsonian Institution, Washington, D.C. Page 79: Norman Lewis, *Untitled Portrait*, photographer unknown, Willard Gallery Archives, collection of Kenkeleba House. Page 81: Norman Lewis, *Composition 1*, Indianapolis Museum of Art, The Thomas Collection, TR10179. Page 88 top: Norman Lewis, *Ring Around the Rosie*, Davis Museum and Cultural Center, Wellesley College, MA, Gift of Miriam Mason Wood (Class of 1961) and Charles O. Wood III 1999.24. Page 88 bottom: Norman Lewis, *Evening Rendezvous*, 1962, Smithsonian American Art Museum, Museum purchase.

PHOTOGRAPH CREDITS

Pages 14, 32: Richard Goodbody, Inc. Pages 15, 19 left, 28, 34, 37, 39, 42, 47, 50, 57, 58, 59, 60, 62, 65, 83: David Heald. Page 30: Marc Bernier. Page 40: Howard Agriesti. Page 43: Ricky Day. Page 48: Erik Gould. Page 51: Ian Reeves. Page 73: Steven Sloman.